Lifelines

Book 2

John Foster

COLLINS EDUCATIONAL

Introduction

Lifelines is a series of five books providing a course in social and personal development for all 11- to 17-year olds. The books have been designed to meet the needs of students from the first to sixth forms, and the structure is sufficiently flexible to allow teachers to use the sections selectively. The books can, therefore, easily be used with a school's own social education course in whatever way individual teachers think best.

Each book deals with a number of carefully selected topics, each divided into a series of double-page units. Each unit provides enough material for a weekly social education session. The activities are carefully structured so that individual work, pair work and group work can easily lead into or be developed out of whole class discussions. The approach is active — learning by doing and discussing — and the activities are designed so that they can take place in an ordinary classroom.

Each unit contains specific suggestions for individual follow-up activities, so that a folder of work can be built up. A number of the units provide individuals with the opportunity to reflect on their progress and thus to take more responsibility for their own learning. These units act as an on-going form of personal recording and self-assessment. They can be used in conjunction with whatever scheme for recording personal progress and achievement a school is developing.

John L. Foster, Oxford 1986

LIFELINES BOOK 2

First published 1986
Reprinted 1986, 1987 (twice), 1988

© John Foster 1986

ISBN 0 00 327436 5

Typeset by CG Graphic Services, Aylesbury, Bucks
Printed and bound in Great Britain by Scotprint Ltd, Musselburgh

Gen Ed.   Health Ed.   Profiling.

Contents

Unit 1 | Friends and Friendship

What is a friend?

I think a friend is someone...

A who will stick up for you in awkward situations

B who always does what you want to do

C you can tell things you wouldn't tell anyone else

D who is about your age and lives near you

E you can rely on not to let you down

F you find attractive and exciting

G who has the same likes and dislikes as you

H who is fun to be with and treats life as if it is a joke

I who treats you like a sister or a brother

J who will point out your mistakes if you behave badly

K who agrees with everything you say

L who shares all their possessions with you

M who will take 'no' for an answer and won't try to make you change your mind

In groups

1 Each go through the list of points above. Put them in order of importance for you, starting with the most important point. For example, if you think 'C' is the most important point, write down 1. C and so on.

2 Think about your 'top three' points. Make a chart like the one below:

NAME Billy	
SELECTION	REASONS FOR CHOICE
1st H	I'm always getting into trouble.
2nd B	I don't like other people telling me what to do.
3rd D	All the other reasons are silly.

3 Now show each other your lists and your 'top three' points. Explain why you put the points in the order you did.

4 Talk about Billy's choices and the reasons he gives for them. What kind of person do you think Billy is? What sort of person would his best friend be? Do you think you would like or dislike Billy and his friend? Why?

Class discussion

Carry out a class survey to find out what the majority of the class think are the three most important things a friend should be.

FOR YOUR FOLDER

Write a paragraph giving your views on what a friend is. Begin 'I think a friend is ...'. Be sure to give reasons for your views.

Making friends

My name's Renton. There are five of us in our family. My hobbies are cooking and disco dancing. My ambition is to be a chef. I go out a lot. I've got a paper round and I go to the youth club two nights a week. My favourite TV programme is The 'A' Team.

Hi! I'm Sam. There's three of us in our family — my mum, my sister and me. I really enjoy school. I was form captain last year and I'm in the netball team. This year, I'm hoping to get a main part in the lower school musical, because I like acting. My best subjects are English and Humanities, and I hope to go to college when I'm older.

My name is Rosie. My parents are divorced and my mum goes out to work all day, so I'm expected to help out with the chores. At school, I'm good at most things and I think I'd like to be an engineer when I grow up. I'm not particularly good at games but I like singing and dancing. I go to the youth club and I've been nominated for the committee.

Hello, my name's Marco. My parents run a shop and I sometimes help in it. I enjoy listening to records and I'm saving up to buy a guitar. I'd like to play in a pop group. I don't like school. In the evenings, I do my homework as quickly as possible, then go out either up the rec. or to the club.

I'm called Lina. I've got two brothers who are much older than I am. They are married and they've both got children. I often babysit for them, because I love children. I'm fond of animals too. We've got a dog and I enjoy taking it for walks. At school, I'm average at most things, but I enjoy the practical subjects. I don't like loud music and I can't stand people who are bossy.

I'm Derek. I haven't got any brothers and sisters. I'm fond of reading — especially science fiction — and I like watching TV programmes like T J Hooker and The 'A' Team. We've got a home computer and I've started to write my own programs. At school, my best subjects are maths and science and I've put down to help with the lights for the musical.

My name is Alison. I've got two brothers and two sisters. I'm the eldest, so I have to spend a lot of time helping at home. I don't mind, because I'm a bit shy, I suppose, and I'd rather stay in and watch TV or listen to records than go out to discos or to the youth club. I like cooking and I like knitting and making my own clothes. At school, my best subject is Home Economics. I hate PE and I hate drama.

Group discussion

1   Try to decide on friendship 'pairings' or 'groupings' between these boys and girls. What are you basing your decisions on?

2   Which of these girls and boys do you think would find it a) easiest, and b) most difficult to make friends? Why?

3   With which of these children would you be a) most likely, and b) least likely to make friends? Why?

4   What about friendships between boys and girls? What sort of girls and boys are likely to get on well together?
Report your group findings back to the class.

Understanding friends

Terry and Brian

I RECKON THEY'LL GET PROMOTION. WHO DO YOU SUPPORT THEN?

UNITED.

DURING THE SUMMER TERRY CAME TO LIVE IN BRIAN'S STREET. WHEN THEY GOT TALKING, THEY FOUND THEY HAD A LOT IN COMMON.

I'M STRIKER FOR THE SCHOOL. WHAT POSITION DO YOU PLAY?

I'M A STRIKER TOO.

AFTER THAT THEY SPENT A LOT OF TIME TOGETHER – RIDING THEIR BIKES OR PLAYING FOOTBALL AT THE REC.

THAT'S YOUR LOCKER AND THAT'S YOUR FORM ROOM!

THANKS, BRI. SEE YOU AT BREAK, THEN!

WHEN SCHOOL STARTED BRIAN TOOK TERRY ALONG AND SHOWED HIM WHAT TO DO.

THAT'S THE WAY, TERRY. GREAT SHOT!

THEY BOTH WENT TO FOOTBALL TRAINING. BUT WHEN THE TEAM WAS CHOSEN, TERRY WAS PICKED TO PLAY AND BRIAN WAS JUST A SUB.

YOU COMING OUT TONIGHT, BRI?

NO. I'VE GOT SOME HOMEWORK TO CATCH UP ON.

OVER THE NEXT FEW DAYS, BRIAN ACTED ODDLY WHENEVER TERRY SPOKE TO HIM. HE EITHER IGNORED TERRY COMPLETELY OR MADE EXCUSES TO GET OUT OF DOING THINGS WITH HIM.

In pairs

Discuss these questions, then share your ideas in a class discussion.

1 How was Brian feeling and why was he avoiding Terry? Do you think he was behaving badly?

2 If you were Terry, what would you do? Would you try to talk to Brian about it? Would you leave him to sort it out for himself? Or would you forget about Brian and look for another friend?

Linda and Jenny

LINDA'S FRIEND JENNY WAS GOOD AT EVERYTHING. SHE ALWAYS GOT GOOD MARKS. SHE WAS IN THE NETBALL TEAM AND SHE HAD A MAIN PART IN THE LOWER SCHOOL PLAY.

I CAN'T STAND THAT JENNY SIMMONDS. SHE REALLY THINKS SHE'S IT.

I DON'T KNOW WHY LINDA HOWE HANGS ROUND WITH HER, THE WAY JENNY TREATS HER.

ONE DAY LINDA WAS IN THE CLOAKROOM WHEN SHE HEARD TWO OF HER CLASSMATES TALKING ABOUT JENNY. LINDA CREPT AWAY WITHOUT SAYING ANYTHING..

WHAT'S UP, LINDA? YOU'RE NOT YOURSELF TONIGHT. WHAT'S BOTHERING YOU?

DO I LET HER PUSH ME AROUND?

THAT NIGHT SHE FELT GUILTY. SHE FELT SHE SHOULD HAVE STOOD UP FOR HER FRIEND. BUT SHE COULDN'T HELP WONDERING IF THEY WERE RIGHT ABOUT JENNY.

In pairs

Discuss these questions then share your ideas in a class discussion.

1   How do you think Linda felt when the other girls were talking about Jenny? Should she have spoken up and defended Jenny?

2   Do you think Linda should have told Jenny what she heard?

3   Should Linda tell her mother what is bothering her? If things are worrying you about a friendship, who should you turn to for advice? One of your parents? A teacher? Another of your friends? Someone else?

Tracy and Sharon

EVER SINCE THEY MET ON THEIR FIRST DAY AT SECONDARY SCHOOL, TRACY AND SHARON HAD BEEN BEST FRIENDS.

THEY WERE PUT INTO NEW GROUPS IN THE SECOND YEAR, SO SHARON BEGAN TO SEE LESS OF TRACY AT SCHOOL, BUT THEY STILL SPENT A LOT OF TIME TOGETHER OUT OF SCHOOL . . .

WHEN THEY DID SEE EACH OTHER AT SCHOOL, TRACY WAS OFTEN WITH ANOTHER GIRL CALLED LINA. JUST BEFORE CHRISTMAS, SHARON ASKED TRACY TO GO SHOPPING WITH HER ONE SATURDAY.

SHARON WAS DISAPPOINTED. SHE'D BEEN LOOKING FORWARD TO GOING SHOPPING WITH TRACY. SHE HAD TO GO ON HER OWN. IMAGINE HER SURPRISE WHEN SHE SAW TRACY AND LINA IN TOWN TOGETHER THAT AFTERNOON.

In pairs

Discuss these questions, then share your ideas in a class discussion.

1   How did Sharon probably feel when she saw Tracy and Lina together? What should she have done? Gone up and spoken to them or pretended she had not seen them? What would you do? Why?

2   Why didn't Tracy tell Sharon what she was really doing? Is it sometimes better to make excuses to friends or should you always tell them the truth?

3   How common is this sort of situation? How easy is it for someone like Tracy to have two friends? Are Sharon and Lina always likely to feel jealous of each other? Can you have more than one 'best friend'?

Problems with friends

Dear Aunt Agatha,
 The other boys that I go around with have started to go on at me, saying that I'm always working. They've stopped calling for me, because the last time they did my mum answered the door and told them I wasn't going out until I'd finished my homework.

 Yesterday, when I went up the park to look for them, they started making fun of me saying things like 'Look who's here' and 'Glad you could find the time to come out and play'. I'm worried that soon they might start ignoring me altogether.

 I don't want to lose their friendship, because I enjoy the things we do together. But I find it difficult to keep up at school unless I work hard, and I don't want to let mum and dad down. What should I do?
 Yours
 Mark

Dear Aunt Agatha,
 A couple of months ago a new girl joined our school. She's called Nadine and we get on really well together.
 There's just one thing that's bothering me. Although she's been round to my house lots of times, she's never asked me round to hers. I've dropped several hints, but she just ignores them or changes the subject. Do you think she's ashamed of me? Should I ask her outright?
 Yours,
 Alice

FOR YOUR FOLDER

Work with a partner. Discuss these situations. Imagine you are Aunt Agatha and write a reply to one of them.

Dear Aunt Agatha,
 I've been going round with this gang of friends for about a year now. It's been a great laugh and we've had a lot of fun together.
 We've maybe done one or two things we shouldn't — like going into a quarry where it's supposed to be dangerous, but we've never done anything seriously wrong.
 Recently, though, things have changed. The others have started truanting from school and once or twice at weekends they've gone down the shopping centre and done some shoplifting. I know it's wrong and I don't want to join in, but they're putting pressure on me to do so. I don't want to get thrown out of the gang, but I don't want to do something I know isn't right.
 Yours
 Jay

What should you do...?

What should you do if your friends start:

A talking about you behind your back;

B teasing you about your appearance;

C making excuses whenever you ask them to go out or come round to your house;

D criticising the way you behave and complaining about what you do;

E going around with a different group;

F bossing you about and insisting you do what they say;

G keeping things secret from you;

H calling you a chicken because you won't join in;

I telling other people things you told them in confidence;

J being unreliable and not sticking to arrangements you made;

K getting jealous because you are being successful in some way;

L refusing to listen to your point of view?

In groups

Look at Superfriend's suggestions. Discuss each of the situations A–L in turn and decide what is the best way of handling it. Write down your decisions so that you can report back on them to the rest of the class.

FOR YOUR FOLDER

Look back at the paragraph you wrote for your folder after working through p. 2. Now add another paragraph on forming and keeping friendships.

How good a friend are you?

Are you a true friend or just a 'fair weather' one? Are you someone who is friendly when it suits you, but who deserts your friends when the going gets tough? Do this quiz to see what sort of friend you are.

Keep a record of your answers and use the score chart to work out your score. Keep a note of your score in your folder.

1 You are playing around at home and your friend accidentally breaks something of your mum's. Do you:
a offer to tell your mum you broke it?
b tell your friend that he/she will have to pay for it?
c suggest you share the cost of replacing it?

2 Someone tells you a very amusing, but rather embarrassing story about one of your friends. Do you:
a tell everyone the story?
b keep the story to yourself?
c tell the story, but mention no names?

3 A friend is always borrowing things, but is very bad at returning them. When this friend asks to borrow your tennis racquet, do you:
a lend it?
b pretend you need it yourself?
c say no and tell the friend why?

4 A friend has behaved in a hurtful way towards another member of your group by making some spiteful remarks. Do you:
a talk to your friend about what happened and say that you thought the remarks were spiteful?
b ignore what happened, because you feel it is none of your business?
c get someone else to talk to your friend ?

5 You have promised to go out with a friend. You suddenly realise that you are going to miss seeing a programme on TV that you really wanted to see. Do you:
a ring up your friend and make an excuse not to go out?
b go out with your friend because you promised to do so?
c ring up your friend and explain what has happened, before deciding what to do?

6 A bully comes up to you when you are talking to a friend. He/she starts to threaten your friend. Do you:
a stick up for your friend and tell the bully to stop threatening him/her?
b go and try to get help from someone who will stand up to the bully?
c stand and watch and not get involved?

7 You are worried because you think a friend is mixing with someone who is going to lead them into trouble. Do you:
a break with the friend because you don't want to get into trouble too?
b pretend that you are not worried and go on as usual?
c try to warn the friend by explaining what you are worried about?

8 A friend has a new hairstyle which you think makes him/her look awful. Do you:
a pretend that you like it?
b tell him/her you think it looks awful?
c try to say nothing or to make a 'non-committal' remark if you are asked about it?

9 A close friend needs some money and, because you have been saving your pocket money, you could lend what he/she needs. Do you:
a lend it without hesitation?
b ask what the money is for before deciding what to do?
c say sorry and tell him/her to learn to manage his/her money more carefully?

10 A friend who is no good at maths keeps asking you to do his/her maths homework, because you are good at maths. Do you:
a say no, because you are not prepared to risk getting into trouble over it?
b always do it for him/her?
c say you will show him/her how to do it, but won't actually do it for them?

11 A friend is chosen to do something that you desperately wanted to do yourself. Do you:
  a make sure your friend sees how disappointed you are?
  b put on a brave face and tell your friend how pleased you are that they have been chosen?
  c try to behave normally in public, but let your feelings out in private?

12 A friend who has an important part in the school play wants to miss a rehearsal and asks you to tell the producer he/she is ill. Do you:
  a try to persuade your friend that it is unfair on the rest of the cast to miss the rehearsal?
  b tell the producer your friend is ill?
  c refuse to get involved?

13 Do you think real friends should:
  a always tell each other absolutely everything?
  b tell each other only the things they want to tell?
  c always keep their thoughts to themselves?

14 On the whole do you think that your friends are:
  a more clever and more talented than you?
  b less clever and less talented than you?
  c about as clever and as talented as you?

Scoring			
1	a 2	b 1	c 3
2	a 1	b 3	c 2
3	a 2	b 1	c 3
4	a 3	b 1	c 2
5	a 1	b 3	c 2
6	a 3	b 2	c 1
7	a 1	b 2	c 3
8	a 1	b 2	c 3
9	a 3	b 2	c 1
10	a 1	b 1	c 3
11	a 1	b 3	c 2
12	a 3	b 2	c 1
13	a 1	b 3	c 2
14	a 2	b 1	c 3

30–42 points You are a good friend to have. You obviously care about your friends and won't do just what they ask unless you think it is right. You may not appear to have as many friends as some people, but the ones you do have can trust you and will think a lot of you. You should be able to rely on them to be there when you need them.

22–29 points You care about your friends, of course, but you sometimes do not understand them. When you are not quite sure what to do or how to behave, try to put yourself in your friends' place. Try to act towards them in the way you would like them to act towards you.

14–21 points You tend to see things too much from your own point of view. This is likely to get in the way of you developing real, lasting friendships. If you want your friendships to be based on mutual trust and respect, you need to start thinking less about yourself and more about other people and what their feelings are.

Pocket money

Pocket money facts...

Most parents give their children pocket money. But there is no law saying that they must do so. Pocket money is not a legal right and in some families parents simply cannot afford to give pocket money on a regular basis. In 1985, children aged 5 to 16 got an average of £1.09 a week pocket money.

The average for boys was £1.10. The average for girls was £1.07.

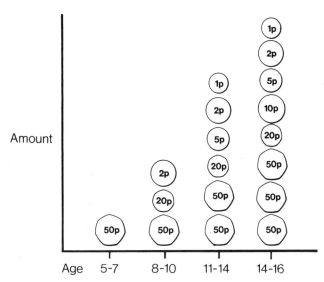

The pocket money table

How much children get depends not only on their age, but also on where they live. The figures on the map show the average pocket money per week of children living in the different areas.

Handouts and earnings

In addition to pocket money, many children get extra money in the form of either handouts or earnings. In 1985, the average amount children received in handouts from relatives and friends varied from 35p a week in Wales to 59p in the North East. Average earnings from jobs such as paper-rounds and babysitting was 40p a week.

Group discussion

Are you surprised by the figures on the map and in the table? Can you suggest why children in different parts of the country seem to get different amounts of pocket money?

Is it right that older children should get more pocket money than younger children? Or should all the children in the family be given the same amount? Should pocket money be given with no strings attached? Or should it be given as a reward for helping with household chores?

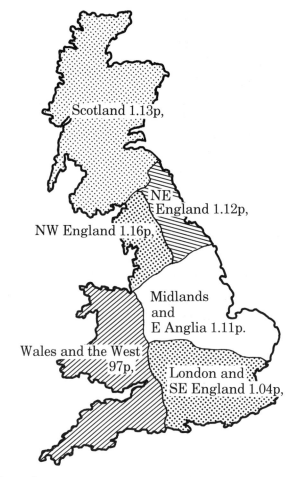

The pocket money map

Are you a spender or a saver?

Dee's lucky day

Dee's just had a windfall. Dee's aunt, a successful businesswoman, paid an unexpected call and gave Dee a £10 note. Dee can't decide what to spend it on.

Group discussion

If you were Dee, what would you do? Each write down five different things that *you* would like to do with a gift of £10, then choose the one you would actually do. Tell the other members of your group about the things on your list and what your decision was.

What do you do with your pocket money?

1 How do you spend your money? Do you 'splurge' it on consumables, such as sweets and snacks, comics and magazines, and make-up? Or do you spend it on entertainments, e.g. discos and films, records and tapes?
2 Do you spend all your money on yourself or do you spend some of it on presents for other people?
3 Do you plan how you are going to spend it each week or do you just go out and spend it straight away?
4 Are you a saver? Do you put a certain amount each week into a savings account, so that eventually you will be able to buy something big, such as a bicycle or a stereo system?

Think about these questions in your group, then each write a short statement called, 'What I do with my money'. Show the statements to one another and talk about how each of you handles your money. Who do you think is best at handling her/his money? Someone from each group should report back the group's findings to the rest of the class.

My monthly budget Date : 1 Sept 86
Total amount to spend : £6

	Budget	Actual	How spent
Week 1	£1·50	£2·10	Magazine - 50p Youth Club - £1 Snacks - 60p
Week 2	£1·30	£1·20	Snacks - 70p Share of - 50p tennis court hire
Week 3	£1·40		Disco - £1

FOR YOUR FOLDER

1 Plan your 'budget' for the next month, by working out how much money you will have each week and how you intend to spend it. Draw up a record chart like the one above.
2 Keep an exact record of what you spend during the month. At the end of the month, show your budget plan and the record of your expenses to some friends. How easy was it to keep to your plan?

Gambling

Gambling is a very popular activity. Each week hundreds of thousands of people are prepared to spend a few pounds in the hope that one day they will be the lucky one to 'strike it rich'. Only a handful of them will ever do so.

Many people see gambling as 'harmless' fun — an enjoyable leisure activity involving a bit of excitement at not too great a cost. But for a growing number of people gambling is a serious problem. These people are compulsive gamblers — people who are hooked on gambling. Many of them start their gambling as youngsters on fruit machines.

In pairs

 Talk about the ideas suggested in the wheel of fortune. What other reasons for gambling can you suggest?

Draw up a list of different forms of gambling. For each form of gambling write down the sort of prizes you can win. In addition to the different types of betting, include various raffles, competitions and games. Talk about each kind of gambling in turn and say what you think your chances of winning are: 1 in 2, 1 in 10, 1 in 100, 1 in 1000, 1 in 10000, 1 in 100000, 1 in a million? Do some forms of gambling involve a skill, while others depend entirely on chance?

THE WHEEL OF FORTUNE

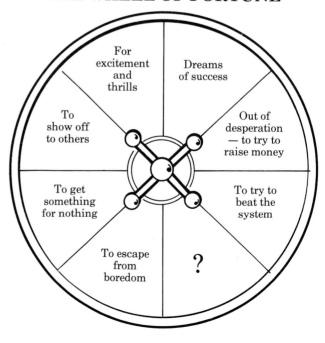

A risk worth taking?

John's Story

At the age of ten John was already on the road to ruin. He was addicted to gambling.

And as he grew older, he graduated from fruit machines to racing. He spent every penny he could muster on the horses.

'If it wasn't the horses, it was the dogs, cards, football, fruit machines, anything you could gamble on,' said John. 'My life became a walking hell. I stole, lied, cheated — anything to get some money to gamble with.

'My parents kicked me out because they didn't trust me.

'I never stayed in one job for any length of time. I was always thinking about gambling and would skive off to go and play on the machines. I just couldn't stop myself. I got heavily into debt, and it wasn't until I hit rock bottom that I decided I didn't want to go any lower.'

John joined Oxford Gamblers Anonymous seven years ago, and through talking to others who had similar experiences has managed to curb his urge.

'I will never be cured but I have more control now,' he said.

Jeremy's Story

Jeremy, just 15, and still at school, had three years' gambling behind him. He talked quickly, his words skipping over the pain, and he was in tears before he finished. 'I lost everything, not just money, but my mates,' he said. 'I borrowed from them and couldn't pay back.

'I even borrowed from my little brothers and stole from my mum. She barely speaks to me now. She knows I've stopped gambling, but can't believe I won't start again.'

Jeff's Story

'I started when I was seven, at Butlins. Places like that are full of arcades and when we went there on holiday I used to play the fruit machines regularly, spend hours and hours on them. I got this craving right from the start.'

Jeff's craving for 'playing the fruits' became more obsessive during his teens, leading him towards petty crime. 'It's amazing how it gets hold of you. I was always going to my mum's purse when she wasn't at home. It makes you lie and cheat, you've no control over it. You hate yourself for it, but you can't stop. It's something very strange that goes on in your mind.'

After spending £350 in three days, he knew he had to make a final effort to break the habit. 'It wasn't just the money. I accepted that gambling was destroying me.' Knowing he couldn't succeed on his own, he went to a special young people's branch of Gamblers Anonymous. With its help, he hasn't gambled for 10 months, five days.

In pairs

1   What effect has gambling had on the lives of John, Jeremy and Jeff? What other things have they lost besides their money?

2   Do you think boys are more likely to become gamblers than girls? If so, why?

3   What is the attraction of 'playing the fruits'? If you had £2 to spend and could choose to spend it on fruit machines in an amusement arcade or on rides at a fair, how would you decide to spend it? Why?

4   The number of teenage gamblers has been increasing rapidly. In 1984 the National Council on Gambling called for a ban on fruit machines in amusement arcades. Make a list of the arguments for and against such a ban.

Class debate

Hold a class debate: 'This class believes that fruit machines should be banned from amusement arcades'. At the end of the debate take a vote.

FOR YOUR FOLDER

1   Write a report of the debate for a teenage magazine. Use one of these two headlines: 'Class votes to ban fruit machines', or 'Class votes to keep fruit machines'.

Money and lifestyles

Necessities and luxuries

The kind of life a person or a family leads (their lifestyle) depends on a number of things:

- the country in which they are living (whether it is a rich developed country or a poorer developing country)
- the size of their income
- the way they choose to spend their money

People living in developed countries (like Britain) assume that the following 'necessities' of life will be available:

- shelter and sanitation
- food and clothing
- transport facilities (e.g. buses, trains)
- employment and, therefore, income
- education
- health facilities

There are people in Britain (and other developed countries) who are deprived of one or more of these 'necessities'. Nonetheless, there are fewer of them than in developing countries.

After the necessities of life come the 'luxuries' — many of which are now viewed as 'essential' by people who can afford them:

- a pleasant environment in which to live
- attractive furniture
- household gadgets
- personal transport facilities (cars, bikes etc.)
- leisure facilities (both public and private)
- personal possessions (jewellery, toys etc.)
- a range of clothes
- books, newspapers, television
- holidays

Group discussion

Here are 16 items you can find in many modern British homes:
bath, television, refrigerator, double glazing, washing machine, three-piece suite, microwave oven, toilet, central heating, electric iron, immersion heater, cooker, home computer, fitted carpets, video recorder, freezer.

   Work in a group. Choose a secretary and draw up two lists:
1 items you consider to be necessities;
2 items you consider to be luxuries.
Then, go through your list of luxuries. Imagine you are setting up a home. List the luxuries in the order in which you would try to purchase them, taking into account how 'essential' you regard each item as being and how much it would cost.
Compare your group's lists with those of other groups. Are there major differences?

'Money, money, money — it's a rich man's world'

In groups

1 Look at the diagrams on the right carefully. How does the world's wealth seem to be distributed?

2 *The £10 million gift*
A multi-millionaire has announced that he is prepared to give £10 million to one of these six projects:
a) cancer research; b) an Oxfam project to train farmers in a developing country; c) a national project to develop deprived inner city areas of Britain; d) world wildlife conservation; e) a project to set up and run centres for drug addicts; f) a project to improve facilities for the handicapped.

Work in six groups and prepare written statements arguing the case for the £10 million to be spent on the project which your group supports. Draw lots to decide which of the projects your group is going to argue for. Use the library and other resources to find out the information you will need to present your case.

Class discussion

One reporter from each group should now read the group's statement to the rest of the class. Does one of the projects now seem more worthwhile than the others? Is it a difficult/impossible choice to make? What will you as a class, advise the multi-millionaire to do?

If there were 100 bank notes in the world this is where they would be:

Africa	3	▱▱▱
East Europe and USSR	18	▱▱▱▱▱▱▱▱▱▱▱▱▱▱
East Asia	14	▱▱▱▱▱▱▱▱▱▱▱▱▱▱
Latin America	5	▱▱▱▱▱
North America	28	▱▱▱▱▱▱▱▱▱▱▱▱▱▱▱▱▱▱▱▱▱▱▱▱▱▱▱▱
Oceania	1	▱
South Asia	2	▱▱
West Asia	2	▱▱
Western Europe	27	▱▱▱▱▱▱▱▱▱▱▱▱▱▱▱▱▱▱▱▱▱▱▱▱▱▱▱

If there were 100 people in the world this is where they would be:

Africa	9	🚶🚶🚶🚶🚶🚶🚶🚶🚶
East Europe and USSR	9	🚶🚶🚶🚶🚶🚶🚶🚶🚶
East Asia	34	🚶🚶🚶🚶🚶🚶🚶🚶🚶🚶🚶🚶🚶🚶🚶🚶🚶🚶🚶🚶🚶🚶🚶🚶🚶🚶🚶🚶🚶🚶🚶🚶🚶🚶
Latin America	8	🚶🚶🚶🚶🚶🚶🚶🚶
North America	6	🚶🚶🚶🚶🚶🚶
Oceania	1	🚶
South Asia	20	🚶🚶🚶🚶🚶🚶🚶🚶🚶🚶🚶🚶🚶🚶🚶🚶🚶🚶🚶🚶
West Asia	3	🚶🚶🚶
Western Europe	10	🚶🚶🚶🚶🚶🚶🚶🚶🚶🚶

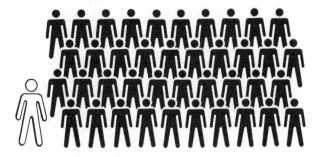

One well-off European consumes the same amount of the world's resources as 40 poor North Africans

Take note!

In pairs

On this page there is an extract from a book on Parliament in Britain. On the opposite page there are three different sets of notes on the passage. First read the passage, then read each set of notes. Decide which set of notes you think is best and would be the easiest to revise from. Write down as many reasons as you can for your choice. Compare your findings with those of other pairs in a general class discussion.

How MPs are elected

Members of the House of Commons are known as Members of Parliament, or MPs. MPs are chosen, or *elected* at a General Election, held at least once every five years.

Today, Great Britain is divided into 650 areas, known as *constituencies*. Each constituency elects, or *returns*, one member to Parliament. There are 523 constituencies in England, 38 in Wales, 72 in Scotland, and 17 in Northern Ireland.

Anyone over the age of 21 can be a candidate for election to Parliament. Each candidate has to give £500 to an official in charge of the election in his/her constituency. This is known as a *deposit*. However, if the candidate fails to get at least 12.5% of all the votes in that constituency, he/she does not get his/her money back. He/she is said to have 'lost their deposit'.

Most candidates belong to a political party, such as the Conservative Party, the Labour Party, the Liberal Party, the Social Democratic Party or a Nationalist Party. A political party is a group of people who share the same views about how the country should be run. Before elections, candidates hold meetings in their constituencies, and send voters a leaflet explaining their political views.

150 years ago, only one person in 50 could vote at elections. For example, in a country constituency you could vote only if you owned land worth more than a certain amount. Until 1918, no women could vote. Since 1969, any person over the age of 18 has been able to vote. Today, the average number of voters in a constituency is 65 000.

A

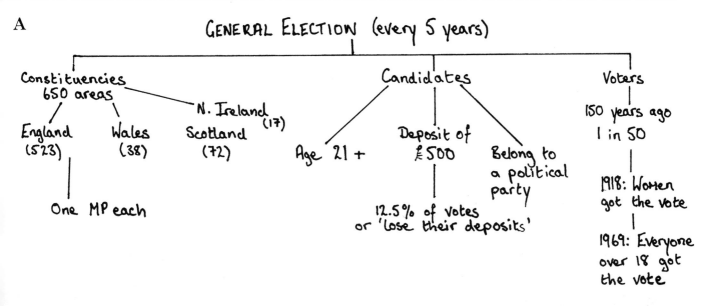

GENERAL ELECTION (every 5 years)

Constituencies
650 areas

England (523)   Wales (38)   N. Ireland (17)   Scotland (72)

One MP each

Candidates

Age 21+   Deposit of £500   Belong to a political party

12.5% of votes or 'lose their deposits'

Voters

150 years ago 1 in 50

1918: Women got the vote

1969: Everyone over 18 got the vote

B

- MPs are elected every five years.
- Great Britain is divided into 650 constituencies.
- Constituencies return one MP to Parliament.
- Anyone over 21 can be elected to Parliament.
- You have to give £500 to the official in charge of the election.
- If you are not elected you lose your deposit.
- Candidates belong to a political party and send out leaflets to voters about their views.
- 150 years ago you could only vote if you owned a lot of land.
- Today the average number of voters is 65 000.

C

General Election – held once every 5 years.

Britain is divided into 650 constituencies.

A constituency returns one MP. England – 523; Wales – 38; Scotland – 72; N Ireland – 17

Candidates – Aged over 21.

Must put down a deposit of £500.

Lose deposit if get less than 12.5% of votes.

Belong to political parties. Hold meetings, send out leaflets.

Voters – 150 years ago only 1 in 50, e.g. land owners.

No women before 1918. Today, anyone over 18. 65 000 voters per constituency.

Improving your reading skills

A textbook or information book is very different to a storybook and needs to be read differently. This section aims to help you learn from your reading by getting you to think about what you are reading before you read, while you read, and after your reading.

In pairs

Work through this section, jotting down answers to the questions which are asked.

Before you read

1   Decide exactly what you want to find out. List the questions you want to know the answers to.

2   Use the contents list at the front of the book and the index at the back of the book to decide which pages to read. Sometimes you will want to read an information book by starting at the beginning and reading it straight through as you do a storybook, but in many cases you will be looking for information on a specific subject, so use the contents list and the index to help you select the pages to read.

While you read

3   Notice how the information is presented. Looking at how the book is organised can help you to organise your own thinking. Many books have chapters or units, which are divided into sections.

Look at the sample page (opposite) taken from *Reading About Science Book 4*. How is the information organised on the page? How many types of heading are used? Pick out the chapter heading, the subheading and the section heading.

Headings are useful because they give you clues about what information is coming next. You can use them yourself when making notes from a book.

4   Think about how each paragraph or block of text is organised. Every paragraph has its own structure. Often, the paragraph will contain a 'topic sentence' telling you the main idea of the paragraph. Study the page opposite. What is the topic sentence of each paragraph?

Identifying the topic sentence helps you to understand the paragraph. You can also use the topic sentence when making your notes.

5   Notice how a different type of print (usually **bold** or *italics*) is sometimes used. Which words, other than headings, are printed in bold on the sample page. Why?

6   Sometimes a sentence such as: 'There are five ways a house loses most of its heat,' will give you a clue about the number of points to look for in a section. Look out for such clues.

After your reading

7   Make notes. Hints on notemaking have already been given in the previous section. Remember, don't just copy. Try to write things out in your own words. Using your own words helps you to understand what you have been reading.

8   Many textbooks have *summaries* at the end of each unit or chapter listing the most important information briefly. Use the summary as a checklist to make sure you have included the main points in your notes.

9   Talk to a friend about what you have read. Say what questions you were trying to answer and explain what you have learned from your reading.

10   Make up a list of test questions to give to a friend who has read the same sections as you. Give the friend the test and then check the answers together.

FOR YOUR FOLDER

In pairs, choose a topic which you are studying at present in science, geography or history. Following the guidelines given, and working on your own, read about the topic in a number of books. Make notes on it. Then, talk together about what you have learned and test each other on your reading. Which piece of advice on this page did you find most helpful?

4.2 Carbon dioxide

Clean air is a mixture of different gases. The main ones are nitrogen (78%) and oxygen (21%). The remaining 1% of air is made up of a number of other gases including carbon dioxide and water vapour.

Carbon dioxide is a gas. Its molecules contain one atom of carbon and two atoms of oxygen. The symbol for carbon dioxide is CO_2. Carbon dioxide is found in air but there is not very much of it. In 100 000 molecules of air, only about 30 are carbon dioxide. In other words, about 0.03% of the air is carbon dioxide. Despite the small amount, it is a very important gas and has many uses.

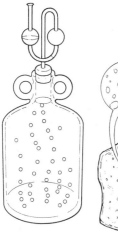

The importance of carbon dioxide

Drinks and bread

When yeast and sugar are mixed together in warm water, the yeast changes the sugar into alcohol and carbon dioxide. This is why wine bubbles when it is **fermenting**—the bubbles are filled with carbon dioxide gas. Yeast is also used in making bread. The small 'holes' in a slice of bread are produced by bubbles of carbon dioxide. The bubbles in most fizzy drinks and in beer are also carbon dioxide gas.

Fire extinguishers

Carbon dioxide has other uses. The gas is used to push water out of a fire extinguisher. In some cases, the gas itself is used to put out fires. It forms a 'blanket' over the fire and stops oxygen getting in. Without oxygen, burning cannot take place.

Dry ice

When carbon dioxide is cooled to about −80°C, it changes into a white solid which is called **dry ice**. It is called dry ice because when it is heated it changes **directly** to carbon dioxide gas **without** forming a 'wet' liquid. Dry ice is much colder than water ice and so it is often used to keep things cold or to cool things down. You may have seen it being used in icecream vans for keeping icecream cold.

Dry ice is also used to create mists and fogs on a stage or for television programmes.

19

Heroes and superstars

Whom do you admire?

> I think the black African leader Nelson Mandela is a hero because he's spent so many years in prison protesting against apartheid.

> Bob Geldof is my hero, because of the way he organised Band Aid and raised all that money for the starving people in Africa.

> My heroes are Ian Botham and Barry McGuigan because they are both tough competitors.

> My heroine is Clare Francis. It takes a lot of courage to sail across the Atlantic single-handed.

> My hero is Lenny Henry because he makes me laugh so much.

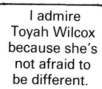

> I admire Toyah Wilcox because she's not afraid to be different.

> I admire Margaret Thatcher because she has got the courage of her convictions.

In pairs

1   Tell one another about a well-known person you admire. Say *why* you admire him/her.

2   Look at the list of 12 people (below). Which of them do you think makes the most important contribution to society? Using the numbers 1 to 12, put them in rank order, starting with the person who you think makes the most important contribution. For example, if you think it is a member of the Royal Family, write: 1. A member of the Royal Family, and so on. Compare your list with those of other pairs. Are they different? Why do you think this is?

Who is the most important?

A world champion sports star
A leader of a political party
A chart-topping pop star
A bestselling writer
A millionaire business person
An astronaut
A television personality
An eminent scientist
A trade union leader
A member of the Royal Family
An internationally famous ballerina
A commander of one of the armed forces

FOR YOUR FOLDER

Put the list into your folder. Write a few sentences explaining the order you put people in.

What makes a person remarkable?

This is what some 12- and 13-year-olds wrote when they were asked to name the most remarkable person they knew.

'My cousin. She's a real daredevil. She goes hang-gliding and parachuting. She's planning to go on a trip down the Amazon.'

'A farmworker who lives in our village. He got his arm cut off by a machine and he walked a mile to the nearest house carrying it so that they'd be able to sew it back on.'

'My grandmother. She had a hard life bringing up five children after her husband was killed, and she suffered a lot from arthritis but she was always cheerful and kind.'

'My dad. He's been made redundant twice now, but he won't let it get him down.'

'A man who runs a garden centre up the road. He's blind, but it doesn't stop him from running his own business.'

'This friend of mum's who is a doctor. She works for a relief agency and goes wherever help is needed most—if there's a drought† or an earthquake or anything like that.'

'This neighbour of ours. He makes this fantastic jewellery. He's got his own workshop and he's ever so skilful.'

COURAGE   DETERMINATION

UNSELFISHNESS   TALENT

OUT-GOING PERSONALITY

In pairs

Read through the statements A–G above. Now look at the characteristics or qualities in the box under them. Decide which quality or qualities each of the 'remarkable people' described appears to possess. For example, for A, you might choose 'courage'. Try to add to the list of qualities if you can. Compare your list with those of other pairs.

FOR YOUR FOLDER

Write one or two sentences describing a remarkable person. It may be someone you know personally or someone you have read about. Make clear why you think they are remarkable.

What is it like being old?

A true picture of old age?

In groups

Which of these photograph(s) do you think gives an accurate picture of old age?

Talk about what's going on in each photograph. Is it right to put old people into categories? Tell one another about any old people you know. Which of the people in the photographs are they most like? How would you describe them?

As old as you look or as young as you feel?

What is it like being old in a world that centres around the young?
Here are some old people's thoughts:

I think young people get the wrong idea about old people because of the media. Too often old people are presented on TV as being senile, lonely or inactive.

I resent the way so many young people are rude to old people. I was brought up to show respect for the elderly. I had a wonderful time with the old people in my family. They knew so much that was interesting and they taught me a lot.

I think it's sad that young people often think of old people as out of touch — with nothing to offer just because they are old. Old people can offer the young the knowledge and experience they have gained in life.

Young people view old people differently in other countries. Take China for example. There's respect for older people there.

I hate the label a "senior citizen". Every time I hear it, it ruffles my feathers. Why should we label human beings? If they feel good and look good, and can carry on their lives, why stick a label on them just because they're ten, twenty or thirty years older than they once were?

I don't care what they call me — senior citizen, old fuddy-duddy, whatever. Labels don't mean anything to me. You're what you are. Just because you look older, it doesn't mean that you are any different inside.

The trouble is that young people never think that they are going to grow old. But they will one day. We all do. I think people should face up to old age.

In groups

Discuss each of the statements in turn and say what you think of the views expressed. Which TV programmes that you watch have an old person in them? How do these old people come across? Do they present a positive image of old age?
Report your group findings back to the class.

FOR YOUR FOLDER

Interview an old person. Before you do so, write down what you think old people are like and what it must be like to be old. During the interview, ask the old person what it *is* like to be old. After the interview, compare what the old person said with what you wrote. Write a report of the interview and say what you learned from it about the old person and what it is really like to be old.

Am I different?

The physically handicapped

These are some of the comments from blind and partially sighted girls at Chorley Wood school for the blind.

'I suppose I should try and understand how some sighted people feel towards the blind, like some are embarrassed and do not know what to say. They're scared of offending us.'

'People sometimes treat me as if I'm about 3!! I'm 13. Some people think you are incapable of answering for yourself. They ask the person with you, "Does she want this/Can she do this?" Someone asked my mum, "Does she want a biscuit?" I said, "Yes, she does please."'

'One of the disadvantages is that if you do something people consider way out then everyone thinks you're doing it just because you can't see, and don't know what you're doing. I'm a Toyah fan. I wanted to dye my hair orange and make it stick up like hers. I went to see her in concert. People felt sorry for me when I told them I'd dyed my hair. And people might think it's stupid but I have posters on my walls and I buy badges and mags. I don't think of myself as being different.'

'If you have a guide dog they think the dog's more intelligent than the owner.'

Labelled

I live in a body labelled 'handicapped'
Stunted legs and arms askew
I live in a body I wouldn't have chosen
But then few of us do.

People say I'm brave
As though bravery were a choice
I learned early not to scream
For mine is an unheard voice.

The world is competitive
And I'm ill-equipped to compete
But I'm no less of a person
Because I'm not complete.

I live in a body labelled 'second-rate'
Though I feel second to none
When Society knows the difference
Then my battle is won.

Roger McGough

In groups

1   What did you learn from the comments of the girls at Chorley Wood School about the way sighted people treat blind people? Why are people often embarrassed when they meet anyone who is physically handicapped?

2   Why do you think many people have an image of the blind as being helpless?

3   'I don't think of myself as different.' Think of all the ways in which blind teenagers *are* the same as other teenagers.

4   Read Roger McGough's poem *Labelled*. What points is he making in the poem?

5   *Can you name them?*
Many physically handicapped people have achieved success in all walks of life — for example, in politics, in sport, in show business. Can you match the names of the people in List A with the details of their achievements and their handicaps in List B?

List A	List B
1 Christy Brown	A Crippled by polio at the age of 7, he became a pop star.
2 Elizabeth Quinn	B Although deaf, he became an MP and champion of the rights of handicapped people.
3 Franklin D Roosevelt	C A bestselling author who suffered from cerebral palsy and wrote by holding a pencil with his left foot.
4 Ian Dury	D A polio victim who became President of the USA.
5 Douglas Bader	E A deaf and dumb actress who achieved stardom in London's West End.
6 Jack Ashley	F Lost both his legs in a wartime accident, yet returned to flying after being fitted with artificial legs.

The mentally handicapped

Many people are only slightly mentally handicapped. They can lead fairly independent lives. Others are more seriously handicapped. They will always be dependent on family and friends.

People act in different ways when they meet a mentally handicapped person. Some are very embarrassed. They try to hide their embarrassment and keep at a distance. Others are too eager to help. They insist on helping them with things they can easily do for themselves. People should try to act *naturally*.

Mentally handicapped people are *people* first and *handicapped* second. The thing is to accept them for what they are. They are individuals with special difficulties, but with their own personalities like everyone else.

The mentally handicapped

Walking
With mother,
Like it always does,
Wading through the rainy weather
It always looks for us.

Running
Towards us,
Hoping to play,
Hands wagging lifelessly,
A sign to run away.

Staring
From the steamed up window.
'Is HE looking at us?'
Eyes that never meet eyes,
Looking from the bus.

Danny Cerqueira

The whole poem was taken from memories of when I was about nine years old. A mongol boy lived across the road from me. I never used to play with him because he was different and I was afraid of that. Whenever he saw me he'd shout out, 'What's your name, boy?' Although I always used to tell him, he'd ask me the same question the next time he saw me. I now realise that his mother must have been the most patient of people. I dedicated the first verse to her because she devoted herself to him and even walked out in the rain with him to keep him happy.

While thinking of that boy (I never learnt his name) I remembered a mentally handicapped girl. Her name was Naomi. The second verse is dedicated to her.

It was one day in particular which inspired me to write the second verse. I was with a couple of friends and we were waiting for their mother. We were laughing and having fun when Naomi saw us. Obviously she wanted to join in the fun and ran ahead of her mother towards us. Her hands wagged when she ran. We ran away from her. I felt terribly guilty afterwards but I didn't tell anyone in case my friends laughed at me.

I isolated the words at the beginning of each verse to show that mentally handicapped people do like to do what any other person does. I wrote the HE in the third verse in block capitals to show that mentally handicapped people have their own personalities. They are a he or a she not an IT.

Finally, the last verse again refers to a particular day. While I was waiting for the bus to go to school, the familiar blue bus stopped in the traffic. The other people at the bus stop pretended not to see the children lolling up and down in the bus. I saw the boy of whom I write inside. His dull eyes were staring out of his hanging head. He was breathing onto the window so that it steamed up and hid his face.

Class discussion

Read Danny's poem and his commentary on it. How does it make you feel? Does it make you think harder about how you treat mentally handicapped people? In what way?
Do a class brainstorm on how people could be helped or educated into treating the handicapped more naturally.

FOR YOUR FOLDER
Copy the brainstorm into your folder and add one or two comments of your own about it.

Smoking — the facts 1

What happens when you smoke?

Tobacco smoke is made up of about 300 different chemicals, 40 of which are known poisons. When someone smokes a cigarette, these chemicals go into his/her body through the mouth and the air passage.

NICOTINE — Nicotine is a very powerful drug. It goes into the bloodstream and at first makes the person more active. It causes a rise in blood pressure and makes their heart beat faster.

IRRITANTS — Tobacco smoke contains a number of irritants which upset the cells in the air passage. In order to protect the cells, mucus is produced. Smokers cough to try to clear the irritants and extra mucus.

CARBON MONOXIDE — Tobacco smoke contains some of this deadly gas which affects the blood's ability to carry oxygen around the body. Without enough oxygen, the body works more slowly.

TAR — Tobacco tar contains a number of substances which can produce cancer. When someone breathes in, or inhales, tobacco smoke, the tar goes down into their lungs.

Smoking — the social effects

YES IT'S TRUE! SMOKING CAN CHANGE YOUR APPEARANCE!

Smelly hair and clothes thats the perfume of smoke!

Yellow fingers and nails thanks to the nicotine

Dirt - well, the smoke has to go somewhere

Yellow teeth - thats the nicotine again

Yellow Tongue - the nicotine and all the other chemicals in tobacco smoke stop the taste buds from working properly so food and drink taste a bit strange!

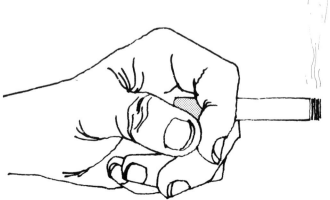

There are other social effects too:

Money — cigarettes are expensive. Money spent on cigarettes cannot be spent on food, drink, clothes, records and so on.

Smoke — people who have some breathing disorder find it very difficult to breathe in a smoky atmosphere. Many non-smokers find the behaviour of smokers extremely anti-social.

Health Service — smoking causes illnesses and these have to be treated. So we, as a country, spend a lot more money on the health service than we would if people did not smoke.

The effects on your health

Did you know?

- On average, each cigarette a person smokes, shortens his/her life by 5½ minutes.
- It takes 10 years for your body to shake off the effects of smoking.
- Smoking can contribute to many illnesses and diseases.

BRONCHITIS — coughing makes the air tubes sore. They start to swell and to produce phlegm. The smoker finds it difficult to breathe and may start to wheeze. Smoking causes 75 per cent of deaths from chronic bronchitis.

EMPHYSEMA — coughing and bronchitis may cause the small air sacs in the lungs to break down. This means that the lungs cannot take in as much oxygen or get rid of as much carbon dioxide. Somebody with this disease can find it difficult to climb up two steps without having a rest.

HEART DISEASE — the nicotine in cigarette smoke makes the smoker's heart work faster than it should. This means that a smoker's heart is likely to wear out faster than a non-smoker's heart. Smoking causes 25 per cent of deaths from heart disease.

CANCER — 90 per cent of deaths from lung cancer are caused by smoking. A cancer is an abnormal growth. The substances which cause cancer from smoking are contained in the tobacco tar which you inhale.

- Smoking can also contribute to the following: hardening of the blood vessels, blood clots, stomach ulcers.
- It can cause problems with pregnancy. Because the baby is linked to its mother through her bloodstream, any bad things in her blood are passed to the baby. A pregnant woman who smokes puts her baby's health at risk. Her baby may be underdeveloped and underweight. The baby could even be born dead.
- Smoking can make the body's defence system far less strong. A smoker is more likely to get flu, colds, pneumonia etc.

Group discussion

Do you agree that people who become ill because they are smokers should have to pay for their medical treatment? Discuss this as a group and then choose one person to report back the group's views to the class.

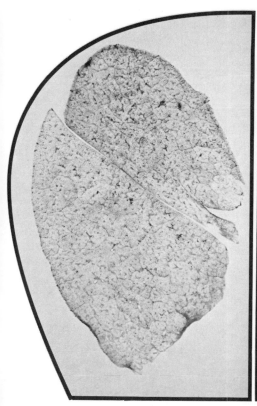 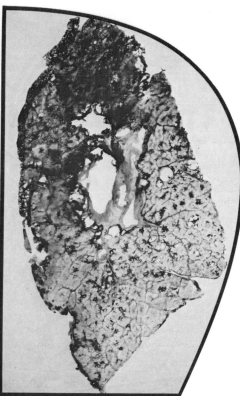

Contrasting photos of a healthy lung (left) and a smoker's diseased lung (right)

Smoking — the facts II

In pairs

Using the information on the previous two pages, answer the questions below and find the words on the grid.

H	Y	X	S	T	N	A	T	I	R	R	I	C
C	C	G	N	E	G	Y	X	O	D	C	I	O
A	A	H	H	F	K	E	C	S	B	G	N	U
M	R	E	B	T	I	O	U	A	A	A	H	G
O	B	V	R	J	A	C	M	R	N	Y	A	H
T	O	I	O	Z	U	E	E	S	X	C	L	Y
S	N	S	N	M	S	T	D	V	U	A	E	T
T	L	N	C	E	T	Z	W	S	L	S	R	
A	L	E	H	E	A	R	T	H	L	Q	O	P
S	E	P	I	E	N	I	T	O	C	I	N	E
T	M	X	T	D	E	F	W	G	H	J	K	V
E	S	E	I	D	O	C	T	O	R	S	L	I
T	A	R	S	N	R	O	B	N	U	M	N	F

1 This organ works faster in smokers and wears out more quickly. (5)
2 This is the disease which most people link with smoking. (6)
3 The fingers and tongue of a smoker turn this colour. (6)
4 This causes a nasty smell which clings to the hair and clothes. (5)
5 This is what people smoke. (7)
6 When people breathe in deeply and take the smoke into their lungs ... (6)
7 Smoking means that this happens about 5½ years earlier than it ought to! (5)
8 This is the drug in tobacco. (8)
9 Smoking costs a lot of money — it is ... (9)
10 These are contained in tobacco smoke and cause the smoker to cough. (9)
11 The air passages produce this to protect themselves. (5)
12 Smoking kills your sense of ... so you don't enjoy food as much as you did. (5)
13 The body of a smoker does not get enough of this gas which it needs to work properly. (6)
14 This is what happens when the body is trying to get rid of the dirt and mucus from the air passages. (5)
15 An ... baby may be affected if the mother smokes. (6)
16 Smoking causes ulcers here. (7)
17 This is the black material which collects in the lungs. (3)
18 Each cigarette shortens your life by about ... minutes. (4)
19 Smoking makes people ... unpleasant (5)
20 This disease means that smokers find it very difficult to breathe. (9)

Why start?

In pairs

Look carefully at this photograph of young people smoking and then discuss these questions together:

1   Do the teenagers seem more grown up to you because they're smoking?

2   Do you think it's possible that some teenagers only smoke in order to impress others?

3   Does smoking seem glamorous, 'grown up', or exciting to you?

4   Look at the profile of Karen Thomas. Why did she start smoking? Do you think it's likely that she will be able to give up smoking easily whenever she wants?

Class discussion

After working in your pairs, come together as a class and discuss your answers to all the questions. Now draw up two lists on the blackboard:
'Reasons why people start to smoke', and 'Reasons why people *shouldn't* start to smoke'.

FOR YOUR FOLDER

1   Interview someone who is a smoker. Before you begin, draw up a list of the questions you are going to ask him or her. Either tape record or makes notes of the answers. Then write a report of the interview for your folder.
Afterwards, work in a group and compare the results of your interviews. Did you notice any differences in the answers and the attitudes of young people and old people?

2   Design a poster aimed at telling young people about the dangers of smoking.

Drugtaking

What are drugs?

Drugs include a whole range of things. Some we all use occasionally, like medicine prescribed by a doctor or bought from a chemist. Others we don't usually think of as drugs at all, like alcohol and cigarettes. But here the word means drugs which are used illegally, such as heroin, cocaine, LSD, amphetamines, barbiturates or cannabis.

The effect of any drug depends on the drug itself, how it is used and the person using it. But any of them can cause problems when misused. (The effects vary depending on a person's body weight, health and mood and the amount of the drug that is used.)

What are the dangers?

The main dangers are:
- Having an accident while intoxicated
- Accidental overdose, leading to unconsciousness or even death
- Dependence or addiction, particularly if drugs are used regularly.

In addition, all drugs can have nasty side effects. For example:
- Confusion and frightening hallucinations
- Unbalanced emotions or more serious mental disorders
- First-time heroin users may be sick. Regular users can become constipated and girls can miss their periods. More serious mental and physical deterioration may follow
- Injecting can cause infection leading to sores, abscesses, jaundice and blood poisoning.

Drugs and the law

During 1983, about 19 000 people were convicted for possessing drugs, and 3000 for supplying them. The penalties for both offences can be severe.

Possession of hard drugs such as heroin, cocaine and LSD can lead to prison sentences of up to 7 years. For trafficking — that is importing, distributing, selling or supplying to others — this can be 14 years. This is shortly to be increased to life imprisonment.

For other drugs, such as amphetamines, barbiturates and cannabis, sentences can range up to 5 years' imprisonment for possession and 14 years for trafficking.

The police can stop and search anyone they suspect may be carrying drugs. But people don't risk prosecution by seeking medical help. So there's no need to worry about giving information about a drug problem to a doctor or to hospital staff.

In groups

Petra suspects that a friend of hers is taking drugs.

WHAT SHOULD I DO? TALK TO HER TELL ONE OF THE TEACHERS? TELL HER PARENTS? TELL THE POLICE? PERHAPS I SHOULDN'T DO ANYTHING?

Class project

A Drugs Fact File

Produce a class drugs fact file by collecting pamphlets and newspaper and magazine cuttings and putting them in a ring binder. Whenever you add a cutting, get the person who files it to mount it on a piece of paper and to write a comment about it on a separate sheet, saying what they think that particular article says about drugtaking. Other members of the class who read the cutting can then add their comments on the sheet after they too have read the article.

What do you think Petra should do? Would it make any difference what drug the friend was taking? Report your group views back to the class.

Why do any teenagers take drugs?

There is no single reason. Most youngsters probably start simply from curiosity, or because their friends are doing it. Others like taking risks, particularly if they know their parents or other adults would disapprove.

Some may take drugs because they are bored. Some because they don't get along with their parents. Others because they are depressed, worried or resentful about family, school or work problems. Or as a 'cry for help' to attract attention. Depending on how they feel the first time, they may carry on if they enjoy it or if it seems to block out other worries and problems. And if they have enough pocket money or other cash — say £5 — to buy whatever is available locally.

But it's important to remember that most young people do *not* take drugs. And of those that do, few will try them more than once or twice. Even fewer will become addicts.

Joe's story

Joe lived with his mother and stepfather, Eddie. Joe and Eddie were never really close but they managed to get along well enough at first. Then Eddie lost his job and started drinking. This led to frequent family squabbles. Seeing his mother so upset made Joe angry. He blamed his stepfather and said so. This led to further rows. Joe felt miserable and resentful. When a friend offered him something called smack (heroin) he accepted. It seemed to make him feel better about everything. After that whenever he felt particularly down he'd get hold of some more heroin — or whatever was available about the street where he lived. It wasn't very difficult.

It didn't take Joe's mum long to guess what was going on. She realised that the family problems had a lot to do with it. She did her best to reassure Joe about

her love for him. She also got Eddie to see what was happening, so that they could work out their own problems. Joe felt happier knowing that his mother really cared about him and Eddie seemed to be trying harder to keep the family peace. Drug-taking began to seem less attractive. Joe is now able to live without it.

Group discussion

1   Why did Joe start to use drugs?

2   Once Joe's mother realised what was happening, how did she try to help him?

3   Did taking drugs help Joe to solve his problems? What other things might Joe have done to try to cope with his problems instead of taking drugs?

4   Produce a group statement saying what you have learned about why young people start taking drugs. Discuss your statements in a class discussion.

FOR YOUR FOLDER

1   Work in pairs. Talk about situations in which a teenager might be offered drugs. What reasons might influence them to accept or refuse? Script a short scene in which a teenager is offered drugs. Decide before you start whether the person is going to accept or refuse the drugs. Try to make the *reasons* why they accept or refuse clear in your script. Role play the situation together.

2   Write one or two paragraphs saying why you think people start to take drugs and what your views on drugtaking are.

Get fit, stay fit

How fit are you?

Fitness is important. The fitter you are the better you feel and the more you can enjoy life. So, what is fitness?

It consists of three important ingredients — stamina, suppleness and strength. These are often called the 'S-factors'. The most important one is stamina or staying power — the ability to keep going without gasping for breath. Next comes suppleness or flexibility. The more supple you are, the less likely you are to get stiff. Finally, there is strength, which enables you to tackle heavy jobs without straining yourself.

Use these tests to check your stamina, suppleness and strength. Keep a record of your results in your folder. Redo the tests once every half-term to keep a check on your fitness. Each time, after doing the tests, ask yourself these questions:

> Am I satisfied with my level of fitness?
> If not, what am I going to do about it?

TEST 1 (Stamina)
Walk fairly briskly up and down a short flight of stairs (about 15 steps). Check your breathing. Are you very breathless? A bit short of breath? Not out of breath at all?

- If you are fit, you should be breathing normally and able to hold an ordinary conversation.

TEST 2 (Stamina)
Run on the spot, lifting your feet at least 15 cm off the floor. Time yourself. Keep going until you start to feel short of breath or tired, then stop. *Don't force yourself to keep going.*
Time … mins … secs

- A fit young person should manage about 3 minutes quite easily.

TEST 3 (Stamina)
Step briskly up and down onto a firm bench, leading first with one foot then the other. Time yourself. Stop as soon as you start to feel short of breath or tired. *Don't force yourself to keep going.*
Time … mins … secs

- A fit young person should manage about 3 minutes of stepping without getting out of breath.

TEST 4 (Stamina)
Stand in a T-position with your palms facing upwards, holding a book in each hand. See how long you can stay in that position.
Time: … mins … secs

TEST 5 (Suppleness)
Bend one arm behind your back with the elbow pointing to the floor. Put the other arm over your shoulder with the elbow straight in the air. Try to clasp your hands behind your back. How many fingers can you manage to get touching at the same time?
Number of fingers touching …

TEST 6 (Suppleness)
Lie on your back with your feet together and your knees up. Put your hands by the side of your head, with your palms down and your elbows up. Try to straighten your arms and legs at the same time, so that you make yourself like a crab. How easy did you find it to get into a crab position?
Easy   Quite easy   Difficult
Very difficult

TEST 7 (Strength)
Stand in front of a wall with your arms straight out in front of you and your palms flat against the wall. See how many press-ups you can do against the wall.
Number of press-ups …

TEST 8 (Strength and stamina)
Get into a press-up position then draw two chalk lines on the floor. See how many squat thrusts you can do in a minute — just as they do on *Superstars*. Remember your feet must cross the front line each time for it to count.
Number of squat thrusts…

How much exercise do you take?

- Exercise keeps you fit and healthy.
- Exercise keeps your muscles in good working order. If you don't use your muscles regularly, they can become weak.
- Exercise is good for the heart and the blood circulation system. It increases the rate at which your blood moves round your body.
- Exercise can help you control your weight. It uses up the energy in food which might otherwise be stored as fat.
- Exercise helps your breathing because it keeps your lungs in good condition.
- Exercise helps you to relax. It is a good way of keeping you mentally fit as well as physically fit.

FOR YOUR FOLDER

Keep an exercise diary for a week. At the end of the week write a comment saying what you have learned from keeping the diary about the amount of exercise you do.

Cycling is an excellent form of exercise. So too is swimming.

S-FACTOR SCORE

	Stamina	Suppleness	Strength
Badminton	★★	★★★	★★
Canoeing	★★★	★★	★★★
Cricket	★	★★	★
Cycling (hard)	★★★★	★★	★★★
Dancing (disco)	★★★	★★★★	★
Digging (garden)	★★★	★★	★★★★
Football	★★★	★★★	★★★
Gymnastics	★★	★★★★	★★★
Hill Walking	★★★	★	★★
Housework (moderate)	★	★★	★
Jogging	★★★★	★★	★★
Judo	★★	★★★★	★★
Mowing lawn by hand	★★	★	★★★
Rowing	★★★★	★★	★★★★
Sailing	★	★★	★★
Squash	★★★	★★★	★★
Swimming (hard)	★★★★	★★★★	★★★★
Tennis	★★	★★★	★★
Walking (briskly)	★★	★	★

★ No real effect ★★ Beneficial effect ★★★ Very good effect ★★★★ Excellent effect

Unit 6 | Family Matters

What is a family?

Points of view...

CLASS SURVEY	A STRONGLY AGREE	B AGREE	C NOT SURE	D DISAGREE	E STRONGLY DISAGREE
1 A family is a group of people who live in the same home.					
2 A family consists of at least two people — a man and a woman, or an adult and a child.					
3 A family consists of yourself and all your relatives: parents, brothers and sisters, grandparents, aunts, uncles and cousins.					
4 A family is a group of people who share all their possessions.					
5 Everyone in a family should have the same religious beliefs.					
6 The members of a family should have at least one meal together each day.					
7 The members of a family should always go on holiday together.					
8 In a family, the adults should make all the rules and should be able to punish the children if they disobey them.					
9 The man should always be the head of the family.					
10 In a family, the brothers and sisters should always be treated equally whatever their ages.					

In groups

Carry out a group survey to find out whether the members of your group agree or disagree with the ten statements about the family. On a piece of paper each write down the number of the statements. Beside every number, write one of the letters, A, B, C, D or E, to show what your own view is. For example, if you agree with the first statement write down 1B. If you disagree strongly with the first statement write down 1E. Then, when you have all finished, go through the list of statements talking about each one in turn. Everyone should say why they agree or disagree with it. As a result of the discussion you can alter your answers if you want to.

Class discussion

Collect all the papers together and produce a wall chart, like the one above showing the results of your survey. Were the views of the boys and the girls in your class very similar or were there any differences between the boys' and the girls' views on particular statements?

FOR YOUR FOLDER

Write a paragraph giving your own views in answer to the question: 'What is a family?' Include your views on at least one of the statements which you either strongly agreed or disagreed with.

Sisters and brothers

My sister Angela

For about two years, between when I was six and when I was eight, the thing I most wanted was to be an only child. I was sick and tired of our Angela — sick of seeing her, tired of hearing her and fed up to the back teeth of having to look after her and take her everywhere. She was really good at getting in the way and irritating me and my friends.

And to make it worse, my mum had got it into her head that Angela was delicate. She was always telling people about it. It was just because Angela had had pneumonia and nearly died. So what! I'd had loads of things like chicken pox and measles. I didn't get so much as a bottle of Lucozade when I was ill. Angela had special foods for ages after the pneumonia had finished. My mum said it was to build her up. I think it had all been a bit overdone, myself.

It wasn't my fault she cut her head open but I seemed to get all the blame for it when the fuss had died down and the blood had been mopped up. I only pushed her because she'd pushed me. And how was I to know she'd fall over and hit her head on the corner of the fire grate?

We were both amazed by the blood. It spurted out like a fountain and even when Angela put her hand over the gash it found ways of shooting out. Except now it went in two or three different directions instead of just one.

Angela didn't cry or shout. She just sort of knelt there looking surprised. She didn't even seem to be in much pain. It was quite a few seconds before I realised I'd better go and get mum.

I went to the back door and shouted for her. She was in the garden hanging the washing out.

'Mum. Come quick! Our Angela's cut her head open.' Then I dashed back in. I thought I was quick but mum nearly got to the living room before me.

'Oh my God I don't believe it.' Things had got worse since I'd gone to get mum. The cardinal red tiles were more or less swimming in Angela's blood and she'd started to cry, and was really sobbing and gulping.

My dad had to come home early and take Angela to the hospital. I just got ignored all afternoon. No one seemed interested in me, not even when it got to be tea time. It was only when Angela was in bed upstairs with four stitches in her head that anyone did take any notice of me. I don't know which was the worst — the lecture about being the oldest or the really hard smacks. It would just have served them right if they'd pushed me over and my head got split open. But nothing good like that ever happens to me.

Chris E. Shepherd

In pairs

Read the story.

1   Is it better to be the youngest or the oldest child in a family? List the advantages and the disadvantages of being a) the youngest, and b) the oldest.

2   Would you prefer to be an only child, one of two or three children, or one of a large family of four or more children? Write down the reasons for your choice.

3   It is natural for brothers and sisters to quarrel sometimes, but many brothers and sisters also get on very well at times. Each make lists of a) the things you and your sisters or brothers quarrel about most, and b) the things you most enjoy doing together. (If you do not have a brother or sister, make lists of things you think you would quarrel about most or enjoy doing most with a brother or sister.) When you have finished, compare your lists.

At the end of the discussion, write down what you think is a) the best thing about having a brother or a sister, and b) the worst thing. Tell each other what you wrote and why.

4   Imagine you work on a magazine answering the letters sent in to its problem page. Decide what advice you would give to a) a boy who has written in to say he can't stand his younger brother, and b) a girl who has written in to say that she is always quarrelling with her sister.

Class discussion

Discuss the answers that you have come up with while working in your pairs.

Parents and children

What bothers you about grown-ups?

> They are talking about something, then when you walk in they stop.

> They are always referring to when they were little. They don't understand it's now, not 40 years ago.

> Some are too strict and beat their children. Some are too easy on their children and don't care what they do. Some won't let their children face life's facts until it's too late.

> They are always talking about stuff like discipline.

> Sometimes they bother me, sometimes they don't.

> When they say how good they were when they were children.

> They drive me nuts. But I love them.

> They don't listen. It's just like talking to a wall.

> They won't let you swear, but they do it all the time.

QUESTIONNAIRE FOR BOYS AND GIRLS

We know that there are a lot of things that we grown-ups do and say that bother or embarrass you. We'd like to know what these things are. Please answer these questions:

1. List the things that bother you most about grown-ups.
   a) Some grown-ups treat children like babies.
   b) Some adults expect children to understand everything.
   c) Some adults act superior and sophisticated around children.

2. List three things you will always remember to do around children when you grow up.
   a) Never underestimate their imagination.
   b) Be patient and understanding.
   c) Try and bring myself down to their level.

3. List three things you promise you won't say or do to kids when you grow up.
   a) I won't tease them because of their childish ways.
   b) I won't try to shelter them from hardships.
   c) I won't try to make them mature before they're ready.

3. List three things which really trouble you about being a child.
   a) It's hard to understand things which your parents keep from you.
   b) It's hard to accept the responsibility of an adult,
   c) but not get any privileges.

Any further comments? Comments about 1, 2 & 3.

Some adults treat their 12 yr olds like babies, they shelter them, and expect them to live a sheltered life; naturally, this is impossible. Parents who shelter their children are being very cruel. If you go to a school with other children, you cannot live a completely sheltered life, so if your parents think you're a baby, but you really aren't, you envy other girls who are treated their age.
I find it hard to be a child, because most of the girls in my class are treated like adults. I think my parents have higher standards than most other parents, and it's hard to be good when everybody else is allowed to do things that you aren't. I have to take most of the hardships of a teenager (12 yrs), but not get the privileges.

In groups

The comments on this page were made by American children. Do you share their views?

1 What things bother you most about grown-ups?

2 How will you behave with children when you grow up?

3 What things do you promise you won't say or do to children when you're an adult?

4 What things trouble you most about being a child?

Think about each of these questions in turn. Make four lists of all the things the members of your group say about each question. Then, go through each list and decide which of the points you have listed are the most important. Use a star system to rate the importance: ***Very important **Important *Quite important. When you have finished, compare your list with the lists the other groups have made.

FOR YOUR FOLDER

Draw up a blank copy of the questionnaire then fill in your answers to it.

What causes arguments?

In the kitchen. The Macdonalds, a Scottish family, are having their breakfast. Sandy is eating a huge steaming bowl of porridge.

SANDY: *(Crossly, as she forces down the porridge)* I'll weigh fifteen stone if I keep eating this mush.

MRS M: It wouldn't hurt you to put on a few pounds.

SANDY: I'll never squeeze into my new jeans tonight. I'll split a seam.

MRS M: *(She turns, astonished, to her 'crazy' daughter)* Sandy Ellen Macdonald! You're not seriously thinking of wearing denims to a school dance!

SANDY: Why not? All the kids will be wearing jeans.

MRS M: For goodness sake, Sandy, if all your friends decided to dye their hair purple, I suppose you'd do it too.

SANDY: Come on, you know I'm not like that. And my jeans aren't exactly rags — they cost as much as a stupid old dress.

MRS M: Don't I know it! Why I ever let you talk me into buying those things ... they're skin tight.

SANDY: That's the way they're *supposed* to be. Except if I eat one more mouthful of this stuff you'll need a crow-bar to get me into them.

MRS M: When I was your age ...

SANDY: I know ... when you were my age everybody wore bustles.

MRS M: Now you just keep a civil tongue in your head, young lady.

SANDY: Sorry. But I bet you and Gran had a few rows about clothes and things.

MRS M: *(Abruptly turning back to the cooking)* That's as may be. You'll have to ask your gran about that — and it's beside the point.

SANDY: But it *is* the point. Don't you see ...? Everybody dresses that way now.

MRS M: Well, I know somebody who isn't dressing that way at a school dance and that's that. Besides, your father would have a fit if I let you.

SANDY: Well then, I guess I'm not going. All my dresses are for babies. I'd look ridiculous.

MRS M: Right then. I've got to get my hair done this afternoon but I can meet you after school if we hurry.

SANDY: At the boutique?

MRS M: At Laird's. It's the best department store in town and I'm sure we can find a nice frock to ...

SANDY: Frock! You must be joking!

MRS M: I most certainly am not. I'll meet you at four-thirty sharp. Now finish your breakfast.

SANDY: *(Under her breath)* Sometimes you make me so mad I could ...!

Group discussion

1 Quarrels between parents and teenagers over clothes are very common. Why are clothes such a sensitive issue? Tell each other about any arguments you have had with your parents about the clothes you wear.

2 At what age do you think children should be able to decide for themselves what to wear: 10? 12? 14?

3 Here are some other issues that cause arguments between parents and teenagers. Talk about each one in turn and say why it is often the cause of arguments: a) your choice of friends, b) your music, c) your hairstyle, d) the way you talk, e) keeping your room tidy, f) coming in late.

4 What other issues cause conflicts between parents and teenagers?

In pairs

Develop the scene shown in the illustration. Act the role play twice, taking it in turns to be the parent and the teenager.

FOR YOUR FOLDER

Write one or two sentences about something which has caused an argument between you and your parents. Say why it caused an argument. Try to give your mum's or dad's view of the incident as well as your own.

Family lifestyles

Helping out

Survey

Question — Do you work around the home (e.g. housework, gardening)?

	Boys				Girls			
	USA		UK		USA		UK	
	12+ %	13+ %	12+ %	13+ %	12+ %	13+ %	12+ %	13+ %
Every day	37	25	13	10	38	33	18	15
Most days	33	46	10	17	30	44	28	37
Sometimes	30	29	74	73	32	22	54	49
					50	45	57	41
Sample no.	57	48	38	41				

In pairs

1 Who appears to help more around the house — British or American children?

2 From the information given in the table, whose lifestyle seems the most attractive — an American boy's? an American girl's? a British boy's? a British girl's? Why?

3 Compare the boys' answers with the girls' answers. Is there any difference? If so, why? Is it right that people should have different expectations of girls and boys? Write down reasons for your views.

Report back to the class with your views on each of these questions.

Classwork

Complete the survey below for your class and then discuss the results.

Housework survey

Aim of survey: To find out how often the members of the class help with housework and other chores.

Class surveyed: Number in class:					
Type of activity	Daily Boys/Girls	2 or 3 times a week Boys/Girls	Once a week Boys/Girls	Once a month Boys/Girls	Hardly ever/ not at all Boys/Girls
Making bed(s)					
Hoovering, dusting, cleaning					
Washing up					
Setting the table					
Washing clothes					
Ironing					
Cutting grass, weeding, digging the garden					
Cleaning the car					
Household shopping					

FOR YOUR FOLDER

1 Write down five reasons why you think children should/should not help around the home.

2 Write down five reasons why you think boys and girls should/should not be expected to do the same chores.

A typical day

Hundreds of years ago people worked from dawn until dusk. Gradually the number of hours spent working each day has been reduced. Now, in Britain for example, people work about seven or eight hours a day and this is likely to fall in the future.

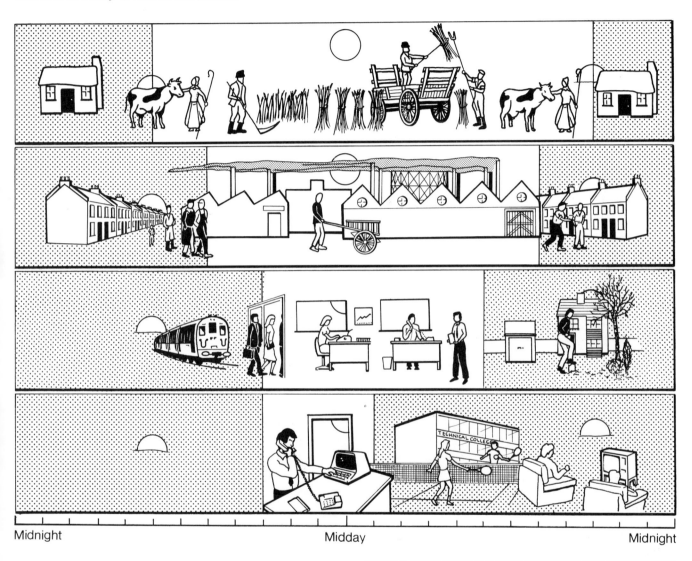

Midnight   Midday   Midnight

In groups

1 Study the chart. What has helped reduce the number of hours people work?

2 Until recently, many people worked a 40-hour week. Now many people with jobs only work for 35 hours a week. How do you think family lifestyles will change if there is a further reduction in the working week, say to 25 hours a week?

Choose a secretary to write down your group views on these questions so that you can report back to the class.

FOR YOUR FOLDER

Choose a country. Find a book in the school or local library which tells you about the life of a family living in that country. Produce a short piece of work showing the differences and/or similarities between your lifestyle and the lifestyle of a family living in that country.

Divided families

Today, one in three marriages ends in divorce. Each year, about 160 000 children go through the experience of their parents separating. Here some of them express their feelings about that experience.

For many children, the worst fear is that they will never see the absent parent again:

I really thought I wasn't going to see him again because the only thing I knew about divorce was that if you divorced you stayed with your mum and you never saw your dad again. I remember actually asking my dad "Which country are you going to go to?" I really did.

One of the strongest feelings about the break-up and the parent's departure is anger:

I've got no feelings for my dad. I see him now and then when he's in London. He doesn't buy any birthday presents or Christmas presents. But it doesn't bother me any more. I've got used to it.

One of the few positive aspects about divorce is that some children believed that their relationship with their fathers has actually improved after the break-up:

When he was at home, which wasn't very often, he never used to take me out and he was very strict and always picking on me and telling me to do things. But now they've split up I get on a lot better with him and he takes me out quite often, and we have more fun. I like him better now.

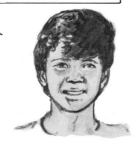

For many children, divorce produces all kinds of changes in their lives: moving home, changing school, new domestic routines:

I think if you haven't got a mum and your dad goes out to work, you've got to help with the housework. We've got our own routine. My sister does my dad's and her ironing, and I do my own and my brother's ironing. Dad used to do all the cooking, he's a good cook, but when I was about thirteen I felt I wanted to be independent and I wanted to start cooking and he let me do bits of roast dinner, and by the time I was fourteen I was cooking the whole dinner when I felt like it. We've been brought up mainly without our mum, and we get on just as well without her. We've grown up pretty fast. You have to be independent.

Many children not only take responsibility for household tasks, but feel responsible for the welfare of their parents:

Mum started going out to work full-time and instead of her deserting the housework and looking after us, she went the other way; she became a super-cleaner, she was knackered. I mean, I'm not kidding, she used to get out the hoover at three o'clock in the morning and things like that. You daren't put your cup down and whoops it was gone. I know it sounds funny, but it wasn't, it was sad.

I said to her the other day, "You want to get out a bit, mum." She said, "I haven't got the money." She hasn't got a lot of clothes and I understand that. But I think she's got out of the habit of going out. Only last night one of the girls from the flats came down and said, "Come on, you're coming out with me," and this woman, she dragged my mother out, and that's another sort of milestone.

Nearly all children say they do not want or do not know how to tell their friends that their parents have split up:

I can remember hiding it from my friends. I used to get embarrassed to talk about it, and I didn't want them to know. I used to think that if I told people, I'd be making excuses for myself. I think I was a bit scared of people's pity, because when mum and dad were divorcing it was scandalous then to have divorced parents. I remember my friend, her mum and dad divorced when she was about four or five, and she hid it from everyone in her class, until I started to tell people that my mum and dad were divorced. I don't think she had any good reason for it, she just did. We both felt we were the only people in the whole school with divorced parents.

For many children, there is the problem of trying to adjust to their parents finding new partners:

I felt pretty jealous. I mean after you've had your dad to yourself for a while and then somebody else comes in and your parent shows their love for them rather than you, you get very jealous, and I got very jealous. I hated it.

I used to hate my mum having boyfriends. I was really jealous. I was so nasty. I used to sit in the room and give off nasty vibes or else make really underhand comments. I frightened quite a few of them off.

Many children feel that the experience would have been easier to handle if their parents had only explained and discussed more what was happening:

I think parents should talk about it with kids and see what the kids' points of view are and how they feel about it. And they should talk about how they're going to work it out and get jobs and a new house. Then the kids will be able to understand what is happening. And they should let them know that other people go through this, because we thought we were the only ones.

In groups

Talk about the experiences the children describe. What do you learn from what the children say about the problems and difficulties which children face when their parents divorce or separate?

FOR YOUR FOLDER

Here is a list of novels for young people which describe the experiences of children when the family breaks up. Read one of them, then write a review of it for your folder.

Bernard Ashley *Break in the Sun* (Puffin)
Judy Blume *It's Not the End of the World* (Heinemann New Windmill)
Nigel Hinton *Buddy* (Heinemann New Windmill)
Robert Leeson *It's My Life* (Collins Cascades)
Frank Wilmott *Breaking Up* (Fontana Lions)
Anna-Greta Winberg *When Someone Splits* (Macmillan)

Unit 7 | Codes of Behaviour

Right and wrong

To tell or not to tell

In groups

Study these situations. First decide, individually, what you would do in each of them. Then discuss your individual decisions with the other members of the group. Try to come up with group decisions which you can report back to the class.

Situation A

Someone has been stealing bars of chocolate from the tuck shop cupboard. The people in your form are all being questioned because the cupboard is near your form room. You think you know who it is because you saw someone coming out of the cupboard when you went back to your form room after school one day. When you are questioned what should you say?

Would it make a difference if:

a you definitely knew who had been taking the chocolate?
b the person you saw was a friend of yours?
c the person you saw had threatened to 'get you' if you said anything?

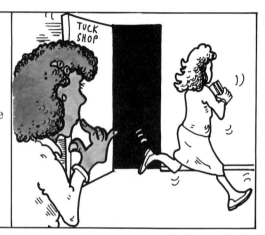

Situation B

You are throwing a ball about with a group of friends near an allotment. Someone throws the ball at you, you duck and it smashes a pane of glass in a greenhouse. You all run off. Next day, on the way home from school, you are stopped by the owner of the greenhouse. He says he knows you were there when it happened and demands to be told who else was there, otherwise he will go to the police. Do you tell him?

Would it make a difference if:

a you had made a promise to the others not to split if you were caught?
b the person who threw the ball was already in trouble with the police for damaging property?
c you knew the owner and didn't like him?

Situation C

Your gran has been losing money from her purse. You are sure that your sister has been taking it, because she seems to have had more money than usual recently. Next time you go to your gran's, your grandfather takes you on one side and asks if you know anything about the money. Do you tell him of your suspicions?

Would it make a difference if:

a your grandfather accused you of taking the money?
b you suspect your sister is in some kind of serious trouble?
c your sister has confided in you why she is taking the money but has made you promise not to tell?
d your sister knows you are suspicious so she has threatened never to speak to you again if you get her into trouble?

Nothing but the truth?

In pairs

1 Carl Sandburg mentions five kinds of liars in his poem. Are some lies 'worse' than others? Put the five different kinds of lying in order of seriousness, starting with the least serious and ending with the most serious. Compare your order with those of other pairs.

2 Talk about times when you have told lies a) to save someone else's skin, or b) to save your own skin. What is the worst lie you have ever told? Did you get away with it? How did you feel about it at the time? How do you feel about it now?

3 Look at the slogans on the placards. Talk about each one in turn saying whether or not you agree with it. Make a list of the statements you agree with. Compare your list with those of other pairs.

4 Have you ever lied to spare someone else's feelings? Have your parents ever lied to save you hurt or pain? Consider this situation:

Mrs Evans is very seriously ill. She has to go into hospital for an operation which only has a 50-50 chance of saving her life. Her 11-year-old daughter, Pat, knows that she is very ill and has to have the operation. But how much should her parents tell her? Should they answer all her questions truthfully? Would it make a difference if Pat was a) not very brainy, b) a tense, nervous child, or c) 7 rather than 11?

What kind of liar are you?
People lie because they don't remember clearly what they saw.
People lie because they can't help making a story better than it was the way it happened.
People tell 'white lies' so as to be decent to others.
People lie in a pinch, hating to do it, but lying on because it might be worse.
And people lie just to be liars for crooked personal gain.
What sort of liar are you?
Which of these liars are you?

Carl Sandburg

FOR YOUR FOLDER

Copy the list you came up with for question 3 (opposite) into your folder. Write down your own personal reasons for agreeing with these statements.

Good and bad manners

A matter of custom

Each society has its own rules or codes of behaviour. What are considered good manners in one country may be considered bad manners in another. A good example of this is the way different societies view belching. In Britain, belching is regarded as rude. But in other parts of the world where people eat spicy foods which are likely to make you belch, it isn't necessarily considered to be bad manners.

In Japan, it is customary to take off your shoes before you enter someone's house. If you did that in Britain you would be considered odd — rather than well-mannered. But there is a sensible reason behind the Japanese custom; in many Japanese homes the floors were made of straw mats and shoes could damage them.

Greetings

In Britain, it is customary to shake hands with someone when you greet them. The custom dates back to the time when people carried weapons. When two people met, they put out their right hands and shook hands to show that they didn't intend to attack one another.

In India and other countries in the Middle East, the traditional way of greeting someone is to put your palms together in front of your chest. This way of greeting someone is called *namaste* or *namaskar.*

In many countries, such as France and Italy, it is customary for friends to embrace when they meet or to kiss each other on both cheeks.

In Japan, people greet one another by bowing. The Japanese also bow when making requests, showing gratitude and saying goodbye. According to custom, a proper bow is made from an erect position with your arms at your side, and your palms turned inwards resting on your thighs.

A tea ceremony in Japan

The traditional *namaste* greeting

Sikh children take off their shoes before entering a temple

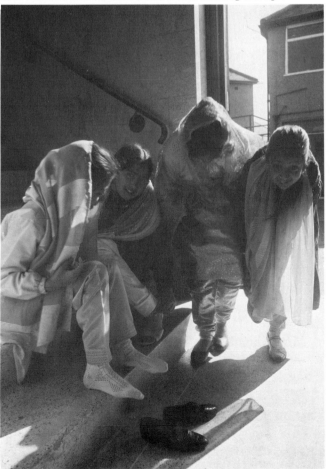

How well-mannered are you?

In groups

Study the pictures. Which of the actions would you,
a) always do,
b) sometimes do, and
c) never do?
Say why.

FOR YOUR FOLDER

Write the heading 'Manners'. Make lists of, a) things you should always do, and b) things you should never do.

45

Homework habits

The evening shift

Sir, down there the telly's on
And anyway it's bad for you
I'm told.
Upstairs is cold; can't think or write.
The kitchen's warm but
Mum will pester me all night
and make me do the washing up.
Shall I stand in the hall
or lie in the bath?
(Sir, it might not be quite
dry, but at least it's neat
— and clean)
Don't worry, sir, I'll manage
Even if I have to
Sit on the lavatory seat
And balance my English
Book on my knees.
It isn't too much to please, sir.
Even though the door
Was hammered to shreds
By brothers and mothers
And Uncle Ted's shouting
'How long are you going to be?'
'Not long, only a paragraph
or two to go.'
'What?'
'Oh, nothing, I won't be long.'
Forgive me, sir, if the spelling's all wrong.

Trevor Millum

In pairs

1   How good are your homework habits? Discuss these questions together:
- How easy is it for you to find somewhere quiet to do your homework?
- Do you always do your homework in, a) the same place, b) at the same time each evening?
- Do you keep all your homework books in one place?
- Do you keep your homework diary up-to-date?

2   Read through the homework hints (opposite). Do you agree with all the points? Which do you think is the most important?

3   Draw up two lists — a list of good study habits and a list of bad study habits. Compare your lists with those of other pairs and add their ideas to your lists. Then, copy your lists into your folder.

Here is the start of one person's lists:

Good study habits	Bad study habits
Keeping all your books and equipment in one place.	Trying to write on a surface that is not flat, e.g. on your lap.

Homework hints

Never try to work hard when you are very hungry. If you decide to do your homework right after school, you may want to have a snack before getting to work. Always do your homework before you get too tired. Don't wait until very late in the evening, or the assignment will seem much harder than it really is.

Break your time up into manageable chunks. If you have more than an hour's work, give yourself a break after an hour. On the other hand, don't break it up so much that you can't get anything done — you should be able to work at least a half an hour at a time without stopping.

Don't put it off until the last minute. If you put off doing your homework, you will have it on your mind, and you won't enjoy your free time as much. If you put it off until the end of the week or until right before a test, you will have too much catching up to do for you to really learn. A little bit each night, enough to keep up with what is happening each day in school, will take the scare out of tests and keep you on top of it all.

Do your homework at the same time every evening. This will help you make it a habit — part of your daily routine. It will make it easier to do, and it will make your free time more enjoyable, as well.

Some sample study schedules

	3:30–4:30	4:30–5:30	5:30–6:30	6:30–7:30	7:30–8:30	8:30–9:30
Tara	come home; snack; play tennis	play tennis; come in and lay table	eat dinner	write book report	do arithmetic	watch TV; go to bed
Liza	come home; read social studies	piano practice	play with dog; visit neighbour	eat dinner	read book for book report	have bath; go to bed
Joshua	come home; eat snack; watch TV	read science chapter	study spelling	eat dinner	help with dishes	work on model plane; go to bed
Andrew	come home; plant flowers in garden	play with best friend	eat dinner	work on science project	work on science project	eat snack; go to bed

FOR YOUR FOLDER

Make a study schedule for yourself (like the ones above) and copy it into your folder.

47

Preparing for tests

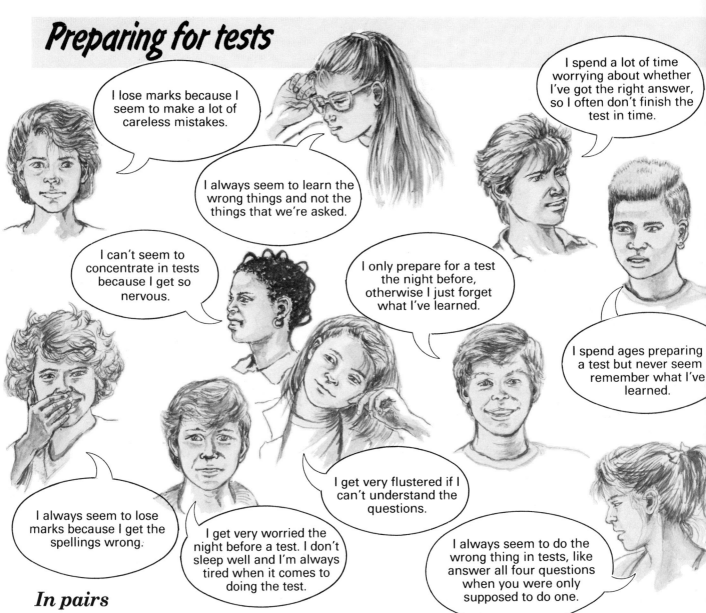

I lose marks because I seem to make a lot of careless mistakes.

I spend a lot of time worrying about whether I've got the right answer, so I often don't finish the test in time.

I always seem to learn the wrong things and not the things that we're asked.

I can't seem to concentrate in tests because I get so nervous.

I only prepare for a test the night before, otherwise I just forget what I've learned.

I spend ages preparing a test but never seem remember what I've learned.

I always seem to lose marks because I get the spellings wrong.

I get very worried the night before a test. I don't sleep well and I'm always tired when it comes to doing the test.

I get very flustered if I can't understand the questions.

I always seem to do the wrong thing in tests, like answer all four questions when you were only supposed to do one.

In pairs

1   Each choose the four statements which you feel best describe the problems you have with tests. Write them in order of difficulty, as Anna has done in the box opposite. Begin with the one you think will be the easiest to put right.

2   Next, discuss with your partner what you could do to put the easiest one right.

3   Write out the steps you will take in the lower half of the box, as Anna has done.

4   Talk about the suggestion Anna has made about how she plans to try to overcome her easiest problem. Can you suggest any other things she could do?

Note: Try to avoid vague statements such as 'Work harder' or 'Try to improve my spelling'. Instead, attempt to make more specific suggestions such as: 'Keep a homework diary in which I write down exactly what the test is going to be on', or 'Find four words every day that I seem to keep spelling wrong. Learn them by identifying which part of the word I am spelling wrong.'

THE THINGS I FIND DIFFICULT   Anna, Form 2B

1 (Easiest) I make careless mistakes.

2 I always seem to learn the wrong things.

3 I get flustered if I can't understand the questions.

4 (Hardest) I can't seem to concentrate in tests.

WHAT I CAN DO TO PUT THE EASIEST ONE RIGHT
Read through my work at the end of a test and check I've answered what the questions asked.

FOR YOUR FOLDER

Put your list of difficulties into your folder. Add to it suggestions for tackling the other three problems you have with tests.

Jed's problem

MS CARSTAIRS: How did you get on in the humanities test then Jed?

JED: Not very well miss. I got 15 out of 40. But I spent ages preparing for it.

MS CARSTAIRS: How long did you spend revising Jed?

JED: Two whole evenings, miss. But it doesn't seem to matter how much I do. I never seem to do any better. It's not fair.

MS CARSTAIRS: I know it doesn't seem fair, Jed. But it's no use just complaining. What are you going to do about it?

JED: What can I do, miss?

MS CARSTAIRS: Well, you can start by asking why you're not getting better results, even though you've been working hard. Any ideas?

JED: The trouble is, the things I learn never seem to come up in the tests.

MS CARSTAIRS: So how do you set about your revision?

JED: Well, I read through all my notes several times, miss.

MS CARSTAIRS: Try working out a more detailed plan. Go through the work topic by topic and section by section. And don't just rely on your notes. Look at the chapters in the textbook, too. Be a bit more methodical. Right?

JED: Yes, miss.

MS CARSTAIRS: Another thing you can do is to test yourself each evening, after you have revised a topic or a section. Use a tape recorder or draw a spidergram. Or get a friend to test you.

JED: What's spidergram, miss?

MS CARSTAIRS: It's a diagram in the shape of a spider. You draw an oval shape for the spider's body and you write the name of the topic in it. Then you draw lines for the spider's legs and write down key words for the main points you've got to remember. Here I'll show you ...

In groups

Discuss Jed's problem and the suggestions Ms Carstairs makes. Which of the suggestions do you think is the most helpful? Can you suggest what else Jed might do to make his revision for tests more effective?

Role play

Work with a partner. Choose one of the difficulties from the list (opposite). Work out a role play in which a pupil like Jed discusses the problem with his/her form tutor who, like Ms Carstairs, offers advice on how to cope with it.

FOR YOUR FOLDER

Choose a topic you have been studying recently. Read about it in your exercise book and in the textbook, then draw a spidergram on that topic.

Wooden tower — Bailey (outer area) — Stables etc

Motte (mound) — Palisade (wooden fence)

steep sides — Early Norman Castles

Moat — William the Conquer (1066–1087) — York (built in 8 days)

You and your diet

Eating right

IN BRITAIN, MANY PEOPLE ARE NOT AS FIT AND HEALTHY AS THEY COULD BE, BECAUSE THEY DO NOT EAT THE RIGHT FOODS, OR BECAUSE THEY EAT TOO MUCH.

Does it matter how much you eat?

Yes, it matters how much you eat and how often you eat. It is important to eat the right amount, so that the amount of energy you get from your food equals the amount of energy you use up. If you eat too much of the foods which give you energy, the extra energy will be stored as fat. If you do not eat enough, you will feel tired and listless.

It is important to eat at regular times - three meals a day. Breakfast is particularly important, so that you give yourself energy to use up during the day. If you eat balanced, well-sized meals, you shouldn't always be nibbling snacks. It's the snacks that can make you put on weight, especially the wrong sort of snacks.

What are the worst sorts of snacks?

The worst sorts of snacks are sugary snacks - sweets and chocolates, cakes and biscuits. They are full of refined carbohydrates! Another reason it is worth cutting them out is that the sugar in them is bad for your teeth. The same applies to sugary drinks and iced lollies. It is far better to munch an apple or some other kind of fruit.

Is too much fat bad for you?

You need some fats in your diet, because fats give you energy, but most people eat too much fat and it can lead to heart trouble later in life. So it is a good idea to keep an eye on how much fat you eat.

Don't eat too many eggs and don't always eat red meat, have some chicken or fish instead. Don't eat too much cream or butter, or foods that are cooked in animal fat.

Does what you eat affect your skin and your hair?

Some people think it does. For example, they say that if they eat a lot of chocolate, they come out in spots. There is no scientific evidence to prove that what you eat affects your skin or your hair. But, people who eat lots of fruit and vegetables often seem to have healthy skin and hair, so there may be a connection.

What is a balanced diet?

Eating a balanced diet means eating a variety of foods so that your body gets all the different substances it needs.

You should eat some foods containing PROTEINS every day. Proteins help repair parts of the body - such as the skin and the tissues inside the body - when they are worn out. Meat and fish contain proteins, so do milk, cheese and eggs and certain plant foods, such as peas, soya beans and peanuts.

Your body also needs energy. You get a lot of the energy you need from foods containing CARBOHYDRATES. Bread, potatoes, cereals and rice all contain unrefined carbohydrates - the sort your body needs. Sugar consists entirely of refined carbohydrates which should not be eaten in large amounts. You also get energy from foods which contain FATS, such as milk, butter, cheese, margarine and vegetable oils.

Fresh fruit and vegetables should also be eaten to give you VITAMINS and FIBRE. These foods also supply you with the small amounts of MINERALS your body needs, such as calcium and iron.

What are vitamins?

Vitamins are chemical substances which help your body make the best use of the food you eat. They help protect you against disease, too. Vitamins are known by the letters of the alphabet - A, B, C, D, E and K. Foods which are good sources of vitamins are liver, eggs, wholemeal bread, fruit and vegetables. If you eat a variety of different foods, you should get all the vitamins you need, so there is no need to take vitamin pills.

What is fibre?

Fibre is a mixture of plant substances. It is good for you because it cannot be digested. So, it helps you to get rid of solid waste and keeps your bowels healthy. Fruit, vegetables and wholemeal bread contain a lot of fibre. These foods will fill you up because they are bulky, but they won't make you fat, because fibre does no stay in your body.

What should you do if you want to slim?

Don't just put yourself on a slimming diet. See a doctor and get their advice. It is wrong to try to lose weight too quickly and you must not stop eating altogether. If you cut down too much, you can make yourself ill.

A balanced diet?

Your school has a self-service cafeteria which offers these nine different lunches. Write down which meals you would choose if you had to select *three* of them. Then, join up with a partner and use the 'Check your meal is balanced score sheet' to work out how balanced each of your three meals is. If you scored 8–10 you chose a well-balanced meal; 5–7 is alright, but if you scored less than 5 you probably need to think more carefully about what you choose to eat.

A

Meat pie, chips, tinned tomatoes + yoghurt

B

Cornish pasty, chips, baked beans

C

Ham and salad sandwiches (brown bread) + milk

D

Two jacket potatoes, cheese, baked beans + fruit

E

Ham and cheese pizza + fruit

F

Ploughman's Lunch – cheese, white roll, + apple

G

Rice with curry sauce, mushy peas + yoghurt.

H

Beefburger, chips and apple pie

I

Sausages, baked beans, green beans

Check your meal is balanced score sheet

1 Add the number of points you have in each group up to a maxmium of 3. If you have more than 3 points count it as 3. Baked beans appear twice but can only be counted once.
2 Total your scores and add a bonus point if you have had something from the bonus section.

	Score 3 points for any of these	Score 2 points for any of these	Score 1 point for any of these
meat – fish – cheese egg pulses group	beefburger, ham, cheese, meat pie, pizza	sausage, baked beans, cornish pasty	fish finger
fruit – vegetable group	any fresh fruit, salad, fresh vegetables	tinned fruit, tinned tomatoes, apple pie	mushy peas, baked beans
cereal – potato group	brown bread, jacket potato	white bread, chips	white rice, jelly

BONUS POINTS yoghurt, milk, flavoured milk, sauce

FOR YOUR FOLDER

Work in pairs and produce a 'Test Yourself Quiz' consisting of ten statements about healthy eating, some of which are *true* and some of which are *false*. Then, give the quiz to another pair to do. Here is an example of the first statement from such a quiz: 1 You get a lot of the energy your body needs from foods which contain fibre. True or false?

Feeding the world

Greed and hunger

'SUE SMITH' (not her real name) was living with her parents in Bangalore, India.

Nearby was a large luxury hotel, just opened. As a publicity stunt it held a 'bolt the burger' eating contest.

Anyone who could eat three outsize burgers in a few minutes got a free pint of beer.

Sue was outraged by this display of greed in a city with thousands of people living in hunger.

With a friend's help, she organised a demo outside the hotel, using posters.

New luxury hotel in Bangalore, India

A young hotel manager told her she was trespassing, and asked her to move.

She moved to the public highway. An hour later, some 'goondas' (thugs) just 'happened' to come by. They beat her up, and broke up the display.

Was it worth it? 'Of course it was,' said Sue. 'I didn't expect to be knocked about. But it showed we'd got them worried. When you see such greed and hunger, side by side, you've got to try and change things.'

Sue Smith's display – close ups

In groups

What do you think of Sue Smith's protest? Discuss these views of what she did:

'The hotel manager was right to tell her to clear off. She was interfering as well as trespassing.'

'I admire what she did. But I don't agree with her.'

'She did the right thing. Unless we make protests like hers, things will never get changed.'

'I don't see what it's got to do with us. Let them have 'Bolt-the-burger' contests if they want. Let her protest if she wants. It doesn't bother me.'

Role play

Work with a partner. Imagine that Sue Smith has asked you to join in her protest. One of you is eager to do so, the other is not so sure. You discuss what you should do.

Factcheck quiz

In pairs

Do this factcheck quiz. Write down what you think the answers are, then check whether you are right. The answers are on page 60.

1 How many adults in the UK are overweight?
a) 10%   b) 25%   c) 50%

2 How many people in the world are severely underfed?
a) 5 million   b) 50 million   c) 500 million

3 How much of the world's cultivable land is being farmed?
a) 25%   b) 50%   c) 80%

4 How much agricultural land is lost for every mile of new motorway that is built?
a) 5 acres   b) 25 acres   c) 50 acres

5 In 1985–86 how much did the British government spend on overseas aid?
a) £110 million   b) £1 110 million   c) £11 110 million

6 In 1984, how much did the people of Britain spend on beer and alcohol?
a) £90 million   b) £990 million   c) £9 900 million

7 In 1985, how many tonnes of cereals were stored unused in warehouses in the UK because of over-production?
a) 1 million   b) 3 million   c) 5 million

8 How much of the food that British people buy is thrown away uneaten
a) 5%   b) 15%   c) 25%

9 How many dogs are there in the USA?
a) 15 million   b) 25 million   c) 35 million

10 How many people in the world do not have a supply of clean water to their homes?
a) 20 million   b) 200 million   c) 2000 million

Food for animals

How much more grain does a person eating beef use up than a vegetarian?

More than a third of all the grain grown in the world is used to feed animals. But in most countries meat is so expensive that the poor can rarely afford it.

Cereals and beans are the staple diet of many people in the world. (We in Britain eat a lot of haricot beans in the form of 'baked beans'.) But nowadays large quantities of cereals, beans and fish are fed to animals. As a result, plenty of meat, milk, eggs, etc., are produced, and the rich are able to eat much more than is necessary for good health.

Raising cattle or sheep may make good sense where land is unsuitable for growing crops. But when animals have to be fed large amounts of food which could be eaten by people, meat production is very wasteful.

In groups

1 Discuss what you have learned about feeding the world from these pages. Were you surprised or shocked by any of the answers to the factcheck quiz? Why?

2 The number of people who are vegetarians is increasing. Suggest reasons why people decide to be vegetarians. Would you ever consider becoming a vegetarian? Give your reasons. Study the extract opposite from an Oxfam pamphlet to give you some ideas.

FOR YOUR FOLDER

1 Write ten sentences giving the correct answers to the factcheck quiz.

2 Write a paragraph expressing the thoughts you have had about world hunger as a result of reading and talking about the facts and the story on these pages.

Unit 10 | Cause for Concern

Vandalism

The street at night

It is quiet apart from the sound of Dan rhythmically kicking a bus shelter.

PAUL: Pack it in, kicking the shelter, Dan. It's getting on me nerves.

DAN: I'm bored.

PAUL: Lend us your dart, Dan.

DAN: What for?

PAUL: Go on.

DAN: Give us it back then.

Paul starts scratching the metal bus shelter.

DES: What're you writing?

PAUL: 'City rules. OK.'

DES: Give you a race.

PAUL: You've got a felt-tip. Y're bound to win.

DES: I'll do block letters.

PAUL: How much then?

DES: Ten p.

PAUL: You're on.

DAN: I'll start you. Ready! Go!

Paul and Des start writing on the shelter.

DES: I weren't ready!

DAN: Come on, Paul! He's winning!

PAUL: Block letters you said!

DES: I am!

PAUL: Cheat!

A moped pulls up.

MAN: Hey up there! What d'you think you're playing at! Do you know who has to pay for that bus shelter? Eh?

DAN: We was only having a race.

In groups

Talk about this situation.

- How serious is it? Do you think the man was right to intervene or should he have just ignored what the boys were doing? Why?
- Would it have been different if the boys had been scratching their names, a) on a classroom wall, b) on someone's garage door, c) on a table in your house, or d) on the side of a car? Why?
- The boys start mucking about because they are bored. What else, besides boredom, causes vandalism — anger? frustration? jealousy? depression?

Class discussion

Report your group discussions back to the class. Then, as a class, think about the questions below:

1   The scene in the bus shelter involved only boys. Is it usually boys who are involved in vandalism? If so, why?

2   Is vandalism more likely in some areas than others? Is it more likely in inner city areas, suburban areas, or rural areas? Why?

3   Can vandalism be *dangerous* as well as costly? Think of situations where this might be so.

In pairs

1 Look at the four pictures and decide how serious each situation is. Put the situations in order of seriousness, starting with the most serious.

2 Talk about the people who will suffer most from each of these acts of vandalism.

3 Imagine you saw someone carrying out an act of vandalism, what would you do? Would you report it to the owner of the property? Tell the police? Do nothing? Why?

4 If vandals are caught, how do you think they should be treated?

'Vandals should be put away.'

'Vandals should have to repair the damage they cause.'

'Vandals should have to do community service.'

'Vandals should have to pay for the damage they do.'

Discuss, as a class, the answers you came up with in your pairs.

FOR YOUR FOLDER

EITHER Collect newspaper items about acts of vandalism. Write a comment on each story, saying what you learned from it about vandalism. OR Design a poster which points out to young people how dangerous and costly vandalism is.

Animal rights?

Blood sports

The League Against Cruel Sports is an organisation which campaigns to have all blood sports made illegal. The Protection of Animals Act already bans certain blood sports, such as dog-fighting, cock-fighting and otter-hunting. Among the other sports the League would like to see banned are fox-hunting, hare-coursing and deer-hunting.

In February 1986, a Labour MP, Mr Kevin McNamara, tried to introduce a bill in Parliament to ban all blood sports. He said: 'The use of slow running dogs to prolong the hunting of a wild animal until that animal is completely exhausted is similar, if not worse, than setting two eager-to-fight and equally matched dogs on each other.'

Class debate

What are your views about the different forms of hunting? Organise a class debate on the motion: 'This house believes all forms of hunting should be banned.'

Work in four groups. Two groups should prepare arguments *for* the motion, and two groups should prepare arguments *against* it. Use the ideas in the spray diagram to help you.

Once you have prepared your group arguments, choose one person from each group to give the main speeches. Two people will be speaking in favour of the motion, and two against. Elect someone to chair the debate and follow the correct procedure of a formal debate.

Enjoying seeing hounds kill a fox is barbaric and bloodthirsty.

Hounds kill a fox quickly.

Being chased by hounds is more frightening for the fox than being shot or snared.

Foxes are pests. They must be killed somehow.

It's a good way of controlling the fox population.

Guns and snares often wound foxes badly without killing them.

Foxes have more chance of escaping from hounds than from a gun or a snare.

People who protest are just jealous of rich people who go hunting.

It's cruel to kill a fox with a pack of hounds.

Following a foxhunt on horseback is exciting.

Factory farming

Compassion in World Farming campaigns to protect the rights of animals farmed for food or clothing and against the cruelty involved in intensive factory farming methods.

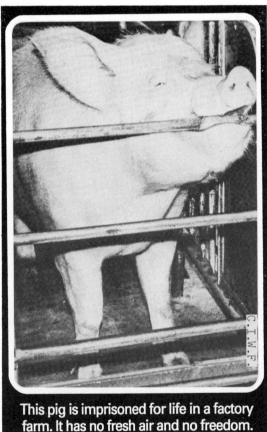

Who pays for your Pork? —the Sow!

This pig is imprisoned for life in a factory farm. It has no fresh air and no freedom.

In groups

Discuss these issues:

1 Should there be stricter controls on the conditions in which animals are kept to provide us with food and clothing?

2 Battery hens often have to have half their beaks cut off to stop them picking out their feathers or attacking other birds. Should battery egg production be banned?

3 Farmers argue that if they did not use factory methods we would have to pay more for our meat and poultry. Would you be prepared to pay more to improve the conditions in which animals are bred and kept?

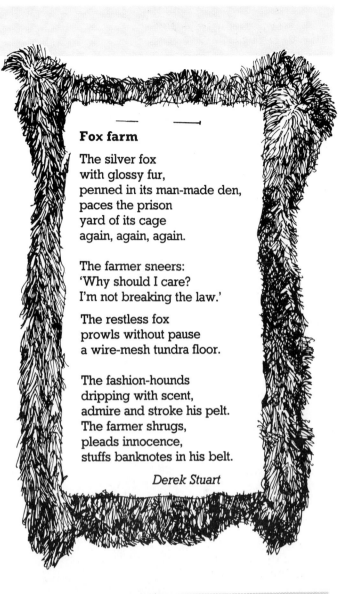

Fox farm

The silver fox
with glossy fur,
penned in its man-made den,
paces the prison
yard of its cage
again, again, again.

The farmer sneers:
'Why should I care?
I'm not breaking the law.'

The restless fox
prowls without pause
a wire-mesh tundra floor.

The fashion-hounds
dripping with scent,
admire and stroke his pelt.
The farmer shrugs,
pleads innocence,
stuffs banknotes in his belt.

Derek Stuart

FOR YOUR FOLDER

Imagine you work for a teenage magazine. You write a column called 'Viewpoint'. The editor asks you to write an article of 150 words entitled, 'What's all this fuss about factory farming?' Write the article giving your views. You may want to argue that it should be more strictly controlled; or, you may wish to say that people who protest are making an unnecessary fuss. Set out your arguments clearly.

That was the second year

What have I achieved?

The aim of this unit is to give you the opportunity to think about what you have achieved in the second year and to discuss your progress and achievements with your tutor. At the same time, it gives you the chance to look ahead and to plan what you hope to achieve during the third year.

The process of thinking about yourself and what you have achieved is known as self-assessment. There are four stages:

STAGE 1:
Reviewing your achievements, using the self-assessment guidelines (below) to help you think about everything you have done this year.

STAGE 2:
A meeting with your tutor, to discuss your view of your progress and achievements.

STAGE 3:
Writing a statement, which both you and your tutor agree is a correct record of your achievements and progress. This should go into your folder.

STAGE 4:
Thinking ahead. You decide what you are aiming to achieve in the third year and write out a short list or paragraph on your plans. You should discuss this with your tutor and then put it into your folder.

Second year self-assessment guidelines

STEP 1

1   On a large sheet of paper, make a list of all the subjects you are studying. Leave enough space between each one (four or five lines) to be able to write a comment.

2   Go through the list ranking the subjects on a five-star scale, giving five stars to your favourite subjects and only one star to the subjects you don't like.

3   Put a tick beside those subjects in which you think you have done well this year and a cross beside any subjects in which you think you have done badly. If you are unsure, put a question mark.

4   Think about each subject in turn and write a comment, saying how you think you have done in that subject this year. Give a reason for what you think. For example, don't just write, 'I think my science is better'. Say *why* you think it is better. For example, 'I'm better at science now, *because* I'm better at setting up my experiments and recording my observations.'

Note: It is important to write what you think. After you have written your comment about a subject, you can show it to your subject teacher and discuss it with her/him, if you want. If the teacher's comment is different from yours, discuss why it is different.

STEP 2

1 Take another large sheet of paper. Copy out the list of skills (below), leaving enough space between each one for a comment.

2 Go through the list of skills putting three ticks beside those skills in which you think you have improved greatly this year, two ticks beside those in which you think you have made some improvement and one tick beside those in which you have improved only a little.

3 Think about each of the skills in turn and then write a comment saying why you gave yourself one, two or three ticks for your progress in that particular skill.

Organisational skills
Has your ability to organise your work improved? For example, do you tackle your projects and assignments in a more organised way? Have you developed a more planned approach to your homework?

Research and study skills
Have you become better at finding information from different sources this year? Are you better at organising your notes and presenting information sensibly?

Writing skills
Can you communicate your ideas in writing better? Think about your written work in all subjects, not just English.

Creative skills
In what ways have your creative skills developed this year? Think about your work in CDT, art, music, drama and dance.

Oral skills
Are you better able to communicate orally? For example, do you take a larger part in discussions than you did last year? Are you more confident about stating your own point of view?

Problem solving
Think about your problem-solving work in a range of subjects — design, mathematics, science, history. Are you better at coming to conclusions?

Reading skills
Has your reading ability developed this year? Can you find information in books more easily? Have you read more books for pleasure at home?

Practical skills
Which particular practical skills of yours have improved during this year?

STEP 3

1 Make a list of, a) any clubs and societies (both in and out of school) to which you belong, b) any school activities in which you have taken part this year (include assemblies, teams, trips, tutor group activities etc.), and c) your personal hobbies and interests.

2 Think carefully about all the activities you have been involved in during the year. Note down your most significant achievements.

3 Do you think you use your leisure time positively? For example, do you take enough exercise? Write a sentence or two about how you use your free time.

STEP 4

Use the questions below as starting points. Write one or two sentences summing up your attitude and behaviour during the course of the year.

1 Have your attendance and punctuality been good?

2 Have you usually handed your work in on time?

3 Has your behaviour in class been good/quite good/poor?

4 Has your behaviour round the school been good/quite good/poor?

5 Have you been in trouble a lot/a few times/hardly ever?

Factcheck quiz answers

1 c 2 c 3 b 4 b 5 b 6 c 7 b 8 c 9 c 10 c

Acknowledgements

The following publishers, authors and agents are thanked for permission to reproduce extracts and copyright material:

The Friendship Game in Active Tutorial Work Book 3, Blackwell Ltd (page 3); *Social Education Year 2*, © Withywood School (page 7); 'John's Story' from 'Play Your Cards Right — Give it Up', *Oxford Journal*, 10 January 1985, 'Jeremy's Story' from *Woman's Own*, 18 August 1984, 'Jeff's Story' from 'Captured by Bandits', *The Guardian*, 17 October 1984 (page 13); information from Save the Children Fund, quoted in *Assembly* by Redvers Brandling, Macmillan Education (page 14); tables from *Learning for Change in World Society* by World Studies Project, One World Trust (page 15); 'One well-off European' from *Checkpoints: Conservation and Pollution* ed. J. Foster, Edward Arnold (page 16); *Reading About Science 4*, Heinemann Educational (page 17); *Am I Different?* by Melanie McFadyean, *KICKS* Magazine, April 1982 (page 24); 'Labelled' by Roger McGough, © the author (page 24); 'The Mentally Handicapped' by Danny Cerqueira from *City Lines*, ILEA English Centre (page 25); wordsearch adapted from *Social Education Year 3* course material, © Withywood School (page 28); 'What Every Parent Should Know About Drugs' and 'What Parents Can Do About Drugs' pamphlets issued in 1985 by the Department of Health and Social Security and the Central Office of Information (pages 30 and 31); score sheet adapted from *Looking After Yourself*, Health Education Council pamphlet (page 33); 'My Sister Angela' by Chris E. Shepherd from 'Me, Myself and I' *Ideas in English* series compiled by Chas White and Christine Shepherd, Mary Glasgow (page 35); *What Bothers Us About Grown-ups* ed. Russell Hamilton and Stephanie Greene, Avon Books (page 36); 'Am I What I Wear?' by Lynn Bains from *Drama Workshop Plays — Masks and Faces* ed. Dan Garrett, Macmillan Education (page 37); table © J. W. Balding from *Education and Health* Vol. 1, Number 6, November 1983, Schools Health Education Unit, Exeter University (page 38); chart from *Living in the Future* by Alan Radnor, ITV/Macdonald (page 39); *Voices in the Dark* by Gillian McCredie and Alan Horrox, Unwin Paperbacks (pages 40 and 41); 'What Kind of Liar Are You?' from *The People Yes* by Carl Sandburg, Harcourt Brace Jovanovich (page 43); 'The Evening Shift' by Trevor Millum, © the author (page 46); *How to Study and Learn* by Janet Wikler, Franklin Watts (page 47); *Teaching Study Skills* by Douglas H. Hamblin, Blackwell Ltd (page 48); *Education and Health*, January 1984, Schools Health Education Unit, Exeter University (pages 50 and 51); *Bother* poster, July/August 1985 and *Where Has All The Food Gone?* Oxfam Youth and Education Department (pages 52 and 53); 'Lay Off Them Shoes' by Harry Duffin from *Lifetime 2*, Cambridge Education (page 54); 'Fox Farm', by Derek Stuart, © the author (page 57).

Photographs

Sally and Richard Greenhill, pages 12, 22, 29, 33, 47, 54; John Sturrock/Network, page 14 (top); Barnaby's Picture Library, page 14 (btm); Popperfoto, page 16; The Press Association and Associated Press, page 20; The British Temperance Society, page 27; The Central Office of Information, page 31; J. Allan Cash, page 44 (top left); Christine Osborne Pictures, page 44 (right & btm left); League Against Cruel Sports, page 56; Compassion in World Farming, page 57.

Cartoons by Barry Mitchell, pages, 4, 5, 11, 30, 35, 37, 55.

Cartoons by Kate Shannon, pages 2, 7, 9, 18, 26, 42, 43, 45, 46, 49, 58.

Illustrations by Annette Olney, pages 3, 21, 23, 40, 41 48.

Artwork by Mark Straker.

Design by Sands Straker Studios Ltd.

Cover photograph courtesy of Sally and Richard Greenhill